The SideRoad
Columnist

Observations from
an Upper Michigan Author

Sharon M. Kennedy

Modern History Press
Ann Arbor, MI

ISBN 978-1-61599-736-7 paperback
ISBN 978-1-61599-737-4 hardcover
ISBN 978-1-61599-738-1 eBook

Learn more at www.AuthorSharonKennedy.com

Published by
Modern History Press   www.ModernHistoryPress.com
Ann Arbor, MI 48105   info@ModernHistoryPress.com
Tollfree 888-761-6268   FAX 734-663-6861

Distributed by Ingram (USA/Canada), Bertram's Books (UK/EU)

Contents

Also by Sharon M. Kennedy

Life in a Tin Can: A Collection of Random Observations

View from the SideRoad: A Collection of Upper Peninsula Stories

The SideRoad Kids: Tales from Chippewa County

Dedication

With gratitude and affection to Dave and Kari O'Gorman who made and continue to make the tragedy of the past months bearable.

Part I:
Memories of
Bygone Years

The Brylcreem Wall

In 1959, a neighbor boy was smitten with me. Every day he pedaled his bicycle to my house on one pretense or another. He might be bringing over a new kitten or returning a cup of sugar his mother had borrowed. Rex always found some lame excuse to visit. He knew perfectly well we had our own litter of kittens, and his mother never borrowed sugar, coffee or anything else, but none of that mattered to Rex.

Although Mom didn't favor the idea of a boy taking me away from my chores, she tolerated Rex because he was shy, polite, and harmless. However, one of his habits irritated her to no end. A wooden chair was stationed next to the kitchen's front door and that's where Rex sat while he waited for me. Instead of sitting upright, he had a tendency to lean his head against the wall. That wouldn't have been a problem had it not been for the amount of Brylcreem he had plastered on his hair. Remember the ad proclaiming, "A little dab will do you?" Well, apparently Rex didn't get the message. I guess he figured if a little dab was good, a big glob was better.

Mom encouraged him to wait outside on the porch, but her hints were ignored. Rex stayed in the chair and continued to rub his head against the wall every time he visited. Another mother might have told him in plain language to keep his greasy head off her wall, but not Mom. She was much too polite to hurt his feelings, so she went about her work while Rex went about grinding his well-creamed head into the wallpaper until the chickens looked like they had been sprayed with oil. Mom loved chickens and our kitchen walls were home to a brood of hens, chicks and a few preening roosters.

By July, the stain from Rex's head was the size of a cantaloupe. By summer's end, it had grown as big as a watermelon. There was no way to disguise the greasy mess. It was too low to pound a nail in the wall and hang a calendar over it and too long to camouflage it any other way. Every time Mom looked at it, she sighed. I think I sighed right along with her. We were perfectionists and everybody knows that's the hardest type of person to live with. We're never satisfied because nothing is ever perfect for very long. Somebody or something always comes along and messes up our orderly life or stains our immaculate wallpaper.

Mom breathed easier when school started and Rex found someone else to court. Although he was gone from our kitchen, the stain remained until two years later when it was time to re-paper the wall. The day fresh paper was pasted up was the day Mom moved the wooden chair that had always been by the front door. She put it in the far front room and that's where it stayed. Never again would a young fellow grind his greasy hair into her wallpaper. The chair was missed because all visitors sat there if they weren't staying long, but Mom didn't care. She wasn't taking any chances that her new paper would be ruined by a boy and his Brylcreem hair. She needn't have worried. No fellow ever came calling after that summer. I went on a few dates in high school, but my callers remained standing near the door while they waited for me. Boys were afraid of me. I don't know why except maybe I was a bit bossy. I suppose some might say I still am.

An Elite Group

Kids who lived in the old days were an elite group. We had no fear of being kidnapped as we bicycled down dusty gravel roads or fished in the deep waters of brown rivers. During the summer, we played outside from early morning until dark when the mosquitoes got the best of us and forced us inside. If we lived on a farm, we had daily chores, but once the cows were milked and unchained, they headed for the pastures where they spent the day. When their stalls were mucked and the milk utensils washed, we headed for our bicycles, the road, and the river.

I suppose referring to country kids as an "elite group" is a bit oxymoronic. We weren't elite in the traditional meaning of the word. We had cow manure on our barn boots, dirt underneath our finger-nails, and no more chance of being elected to political office than the chickens in our coops had of flying to the treetops. We recognized the sulfurous odor if a hen was in a broody mood and sat too long on her unfertilized eggs. We had scratches and scrapes on our knees and elbows when our bicycles hit a rut and threw us on the gravel road.

Boys caught suckers with a worm dangling from a makeshift hook attached to a piece of string tied to a stick. There were no fancy fishing poles with expensive reels and exotic lures. Girls played with dolls, read Little Golden Books, and waited for wild berries to ripen in the fields outside our front doors. When boys got tired of fishing, they played with plastic soldiers or cowboys. When girls got tired, we got out crayons and coloring books.

Forts were built from dead tree limbs dragged from the woods. Leafy branches from live trees comprised the walls. In a pinch, blankets were thrown over the clotheslines and became tents where plans were hatched to thwart an approaching enemy. Boys spent nights in empty haymows as mice tickled their noses. Girls spent hours in their playhouse preparing pretend meals and playing dress-up. Riding bikes was a mandatory activity for both boys and girls. Nobody had a new bicycle. Everybody made do with bikes too small, too big, too old, and too ugly. Nobody laughed because the make and model wasn't important. It was the freedom it afforded.

Although we never traveled far from home, our imaginations took us miles from our sideroad. We could be anybody, anywhere, including the heroines and heroes we read about in books and comics. In the early days of our youth, nobody owned a television or telephone. We played, we dreamed, we lived in a world of our imagination, and we were all the better for it.

Summer Softball Games

The summer hours of daylight last long into the evening and remind me of the days when we played softball until the mosquitoes got so thick we couldn't see the bases. We were a motley group with no more batting, catching or outfielding ability than our dogs. What we did have was a love of the game. When the school year was over, our front yard became the ball diamond. The players were my siblings, one cousin, and the boys who lived north of us. Occasionally the kids who lived down the road joined in. Their parents rented the house south of our place so we considered them nesters, not permanent residents.

Sometimes we coaxed my parents into taking a turn at bat for each side. Mom would hit the ball to the left and surprise the outfielder who was standing to the right. Everybody loved Dad's line drives and pop-up flies because if a fielder was any good at all, he could catch them. When we heard the crack of the bat as it connected with the ball, one of us kids would run for first base. We knew there wasn't a chance of anyone catching Mom's hit, and we hoped a fielder would drop one of Dad's.

Every major league team has a pre-game ritual and we were no different. Roger climbed our maple tree and hung from his knees. This dare-devil feat was never mastered by anyone else, either through fear of falling or out of respect for Roger. Once he climbed down, we began the battle to see who was up first. Our style was a little different from the Tigers'. We simply picked a member of each team, and the hand that landed on the top of the bat had first ups.

Nobody had a glove, at least not during the first few games. I think one appeared at some point, but it might have been a lefty because if an outfielder had the good luck to catch the ball, it immediately rolled out of the glove and unto the grass. The batter was safe, and a cheer went up from the kids at home plate. The glove was discarded as a useless piece of leather destined to outwit anyone who wore it.

In those days, nobody had money for fancy equipment. The glove was probably fished out of an old barrel in someone's garage or barn. Our bases were anything handy. They might have been stones or pieces of wood. There was no definite distance between bases. We spaced them as far apart as we thought necessary. Third was usually closer to home than first was to second. If one of our dogs was feeling frisky, it wasn't uncommon for him to pick up a base and carry it away.

Rex was the home run hitter. One swing of the bat and we knew he didn't have to run. He could take his time as he walked the bases while an outfielder crossed the road to find the ball. Sometimes it landed among the weeds in the ditch. Other times it disappeared completely and we resorted to the wiffle ball. I loved that ball because it was much easier to hit than the regular softball.

We laughed, we yelled, we argued, and we played as if that summer would never end. It did, of course, as all summers must end, but it left enough memories for a lifetime. Now when I see the sun bidding farewell to the day, I recall the summer of 1958 when the sun dipped low, our game ended, and the sideroad kids went home.

Siblings and a City Dog

Jude did her best to entertain my brother, Ed, and me, but she wasn't always successful. Asking us to climb in a wagon is one example of a "good time" that backfired. She probably intended to pull us up and down our lane or maybe even down the road and pretend we were having an adventure, but the last place Ed and I wanted to be was in a Service Truck wagon. I'm sure he would have preferred to build roads in our sandbox, and I wanted to be in the house where my dolls were waiting for me and the tea party I had promised them.

Occasionally Jude and I deserted our brother and walked across the road to Uncle Steve's home, especially when our aunt and uncle from Detroit visited for two weeks during the summer. They had no offspring so their dog, Topsy, was as spoiled as a child without siblings. We were allowed to play with her if we promised no rough-housing. At the first whimper of distress, we were told to go home and not come back until we knew how to treat a "city" dog.

Jude scoffed at the very idea. City dog, indeed. The older she got, the more she preferred our dogs, Pepper and Sparky, who loved to roll in cow manure, chase the cats, and act like perfectly normal country dogs. Naturally, she wouldn't have dreamed of telling our Detroit relatives that she considered Topsy a sissy, a crybaby, and a thorough disgrace to the canine kingdom. When she died at the ripe old age of fifteen, Uncle Francis was lost without her, but Jude and I were not. We'd had enough of a dog that wore ribbons in her hair and preferred a bowl of expensive food to a fresh bone from the butcher shop.

Topsy was the only city dog we ever knew. My aunt and uncle felt it would be unkind to her memory if another dog replaced her.

It's Gonna Be a Scorcher

In the old days, we were told to head for the river after we finished our morning chores because it was gonna be a scorcher. The best way to stay cool was to swim among the yellow lily pads in the river's lovely cold water. Unfortunately, there was no efficient way to cool the house other than putting screens in the windows, and all that did was let in more hot air. The screens were surrounded by a wooden frame and adjusted to fit the window. As well as letting in the heat, they weren't very effective in keeping out flies and mosquitoes. When the day waned and a cool breeze blew through them, they did aid in cooling the downstairs rooms, but they didn't give much relief to the upstairs bedrooms.

Keeping cool in the car was a real challenge. Naturally, we rolled down the windows but that created another problem. Our sideroad and Six Mile Road were not paved. A five-mile trip to Brimley on scorcher Sunday mornings meant we choked on dust filling the car. When we could no longer breathe, we rolled up the windows and roasted. Dad smoked in those days, so along with dust in our lungs, we inhaled puffs of unfiltered Camels. By the time we got to church, our clothes were dusty, our throats were parched, our parents were arguing, and we dreaded the hour we would spend listening to the priest yell at us.

Scorchers had the ability to bring out the worst in people. Mom used to say we could pile on the clothes in cold weather, but there was only so much we could take off during a hot spell. Of course, this is no longer true. Women now parade around in skimpy outfits and men strip down to Bermuda shorts and sandals. People were modest in the old days. Gals were horrified if their bra strap was visible or their slip showed. Fellows kept their hairy chests, knobby knees, bony legs, and chipped toenails well under cover.

We either had more self-respect in the old days or we were incredibly dumb. Most country kids minded our parents. It was drilled into girls to act "lady-like." For me, that meant wearing clothing that concealed everything. I had more pedal pushers than shorts and more long-sleeved blouses than sleeveless ones. The hemlines of my skirts and dresses were well below my knees. Every button on my blouse was buttoned. Even during a scorcher, I preferred to stay indoors and read rather than venture outside without the cover of plaid shirts and overalls.

I shudder to think what scorchers will do to people in the future. Those who have no air conditioning in their homes or vehicles will melt like ice cream cones in ninety-degree weather. Tempers will rise to the boiling point. And kids who once would have taken to neighborhood rivers will stay locked in their bedrooms, oblivious to everything but the electronic screens in front of them.

The Wounds of Youth

Many years ago, my brother and I were fighting over a pencil. I remember the event as if it happened yesterday because it was the only argument in which one of us sustained an injury. Usually we fought with words. Nothing bad, of course, but since we listened to a fire and brimstone priest every Sunday, the worst we came up with was threatening each other with hellfire. I can't imagine kids doing that today, but in the old days hell was as real to us as the cows in our pasture.

I had just sharpened a pencil to finish a project I was working on. Mom had purchased a set of workbooks and encouraged us to play "school" during summer so we wouldn't forget everything we had learned during our nine months of educational confinement. Arithmetic and spelling were at the top of the list as were books full of mazes and puzzles to hone our critical thinking skills. We didn't know what "critical thinking" meant, but we had fun finding our way out of a maze or following the dots to see what we had created.

Anyway, instead of sitting at the table, I had chosen the purple couch in the far front room and put the workbook on my lap. Ed wanted my pencil. I don't remember if the point on his was dull or if it was too short to sharpen. Being an inconsiderate older sister, I said no and that's when the struggle began. My brother grabbed the eraser end, and I clung to the pointy end. We were quite young, our hands were small, the pencil was sharp, and the fight was on.

It didn't last long. I have no analytical ability. It never occurred to me that if he let go, the freshly sharpened pencil I was determined to hold on to would puncture my thigh. Although my brother was two years my junior, he was very clever. He realized I would never relinquish my hold so he relinquished his. When he gave up, the force of thrust caused me to stab myself with the sharp end. To this day, the bit of graphite that went through my pedal pushers and lodged in my left inner thigh is still there.

Naturally, I howled like a wolf baying at the moon. Mom ran from the kitchen and inspected the wound. She said I would live and returned to the kitchen. Ed magically disappeared, and my sister was not home. I was left alone to nurse the puncture wound and feel sorry for myself, a youthful trait some relatives say I never left in childhood. What got me thinking about the pencil fight was the realization that the speck of graphite is no longer visible. Its disappearance wasn't the result of surgical removal, but of weight gain. Now that my thighs are much larger, the proof of a childhood scrimmage is history.

And so it goes. We age, we change, but we never forget the pencil fight when we were scarred for life until weight gain hid any trace that the battle ever occurred.

Cows on the Road

Recently, I was returning home from Sault Ste. Marie via Six Mile Road and noticed cars were slowing down as they neared an Amish farm. When I approached, it became obvious what was causing the commotion. Three Black Angus had walked through the fence, crossed the ditch, and were strolling down the road. A young Amish boy was trying to herd the cattle back through the hole from which they had escaped.

It took only a moment to pass by and continue on my way so I have no idea how much luck he had in corralling his charges, but the sight brought back memories from when I was young. On summer afternoons, it wasn't uncommon to see milk cows on the road. In the old days, such animals were essential to anyone living on a farm. Cows were social creatures. If they saw a downed barbed wire fence, they took advantage of it and made the rounds. In other words, they visited neighboring bovines.

When we saw cows on the loose, we knew they belonged to the neighbors who lived south or north of us. It didn't take long to get a switch, turn the cows around and walk them back to their own barnyard. However, if we didn't recognize the bossies, we knew they had meandered from one road over. In olden days, the fields were not overgrown so once the cows were free, they easily traveled a mile or two without undue hindrance. Away from their own pastures, they could sample fresh grass, sip a cool drink from the river and continue on their adventure. They feared nothing. If a dog chased them, they'd land a kick on its nose and that was the end of the chase. Usually, no more than four dairy cows made the trip. The others had the good sense to stay put, enjoy their own grass and seek shelter from the afternoon sun in their own woods. Eventually the owner of the wayward cows would come looking for them, round them up and walk them home.

In an old picture album, there are photographs of our Herefords in the front yard of Bill Sarley's home. Our beef cattle pastured down the road from us. They had eighty acres in which to roam, but maybe they were bored and wanted to journey beyond their familiar confines. Bill's house was only a short distance away. When he saw the cattle grazing on his grass, he walked to our place and told my parents where their Herefords were having lunch. Dad got in his truck and drove Bill home. I don't know which one snapped the photos or how long it took them to round up the cows, but the pictures tell the story of two men sitting on a bench and enjoying a beer before tending to the Herefords.

Such was life in the 1950s when cows and men got along.

The TV is Snowy

Dad bought our first television in 1957. When it was deposited in our front room and plugged in, the event was as momentous as the moon landing. However, it was a Herculean task to adjust the outside antenna until it delivered something other than snow to the screen. Dad climbed a ladder to the roof and fiddled with the antenna. We ran to our posts. Mom watched the screen and alerted us when the snow disappeared and a picture appeared. Ed stood at the kitchen door and yelled the good news to me. From the back shed, I yelled to my sister who stood outside. She yelled to Dad, and he descended the ladder. Success had been achieved.

I don't remember the picture being perfectly clear because there was always a hint of snow, but it didn't bother us. Chores were temporarily forgotten and popcorn was popped. We plunked in our favorite chairs and glued our eyes to the screen, hoping something other than the test pattern would miraculously appear.

In the early days, there was no such thing as color, so naturally all the shows were in black-and-white. I have no recollection of the first program we watched, but I do remember comics like Red Skelton and Jack Benny. The only children's show that comes to mind is Buffalo Bob's "Howdy Doody." Howdy was as memorable a character as Dilly Dally, Mr. Bluster, and Clarabell the Clown.

Initially our antenna pulled in only one channel, NBC. I'm not sure when we watched our first Canadian show. What I remember most is the constant struggle to eliminate snow from the screen. All it took was a strong gust of wind to turn the antenna in the wrong direction and create a snowstorm. Then like soldiers, we manned our posts and repeated the drill. Dad climbed the ladder regardless of the season or weather conditions. Unless there was a raging snowstorm, he was up the ladder and on the roof until he heard the glorious shout, "Stop. That's perfect. The snow is gone."

Rabbit ears were standard issue with early televisions and sat on top of the TV. They were pretty much useless, thus the need for the outside antenna. When my folks moved into their mobile home, the antenna came with them. Dad disassembled it and attached it to a pole, then ran a grounding line. From 1968 onward, he never again had to climb a ladder and stand on the roof. Television snow was only a memory, but in retrospect, what a special memory it was.

Time to Get out the Butter Knife

When autumn winds blew into November, it was time to batten the hatches and hunker down. Along with the usual supply of wood for the kitchen stove and bales of hay banked against the side of the house, we checked the rag bag and picked out the best ones. We also kept a butter knife handy. Our farmhouse was old and drafty. Wind found its way around or underneath any door or window crack. Our front door was especially ill-fitting.

It was Mom's custom to plug the space between the door and the wall. Each night before she went to bed, she pushed rags into the gap with the aid of the butter knife. Although nothing could keep the cold at bay once the wood in the stove burned out, the rags discouraged wind from entering the kitchen. Often an old blanket was hung over the front door to further prevent invasion of the elements. Every night until spring, the butter knife was jammed through the blanket and rags. If it was a particularly cold day, the rags and knife stayed in place and we entered and left by the back door.

Winters were not easy in a house with no furnace. Getting up in the morning took real courage. A stovepipe ran from the Jungers oil heater in the front room to the upstairs hall and made a pathetic attempt to take the chill off the bedrooms. Mom used to say that on especially arctic nights the milk in our baby bottle froze. It's a wonder we didn't perish from the cold as infants, but we were hardy. When I was a teenager, I wrapped my school clothes around the stovepipe in an attempt to warm them. I kept my winter boots behind the kitchen stove next to the cat's basket and rested my mittens or gloves on the Jungers for a few minutes before I ventured outside.

A bitterly cold night meant water in the kitchen pails had a thin layer of ice on them which had to be cracked in the morning and heated before we washed. Our washstand wasn't fancy. It was a slab of wood nailed to four birch boughs. A piece of yellow oilcloth covered it. Every morning before school, we scrubbed our faces, necks, elbows, and hands in the wash dish. We checked our appearance in the white medicine cabinet nailed above the washstand. Unlike siblings of today, we never fought over who got the bathroom first because there wasn't one. We had a choice between the upstairs commode or the outhouse.

Until I was twenty-one, I lived much as generations before me. Like my parents, I learned to survive without many frills. We were well-acquainted with the galvanized washtub, winter clotheslines strung in the front room, and constantly feeling cold. Occasionally, the oil stove would go out during the night, and the house would be freezing. Dad would have to get up and fuss with it until the blue and orange flames jumped to life. That was a welcome sight.

With few exceptions, generations that came after me are unacquainted with the old way of life. They can't imagine a world without modern conveniences. Magazines like "Country Living" paint a glowing picture of country life, but we old-timers know the truth. It was a hard existence, but we survived and are willing to tell our story to anyone willing to listen.

Deer Season and the Woodshed

When I was young, my uncles and older cousins gathered at our house on the first day of deer hunting season. The first light of dawn saw the men drinking hot coffee around our kitchen table and making plans for the day. Although there were always disagreements about who would watch where, the men enjoyed hunting and the camaraderie it inspired. My cousins grumbled about driving the woods, but every November they showed up early and stayed late. I don't know why everybody congregated at our house unless it was to eat a couple of Gram's cinnamon rolls hot from the oven, or a warm scone slathered with Mom's strawberry jam.

There was always plenty of snow. The men dressed in red and black woolen plaid jackets, pants and hats. They all wore heavy woolen socks and green rubber boots with laces. Unlike today, the hunting actually took place in the woods, not in the back yard where a pile of carrots or corn make for an easy kill. My cousins were the hounds. It fell to them to drive the bush and chase deer into the open where an experienced parent or uncle sat watch. Once a deer was in sight, the older fellow picked it off. If the deer was wounded but did not fall, the younger boys tracked it and finished the job which gave them bragging rights.

Mom took pictures of proud hunters standing in front of the deer hanging from the maple tree in our front yard. In those days the temperature was always cold enough to freeze the carcass. A few times during the season I recall hearing about "the one in the wood shed" but I never questioned why it was in the shed instead of swinging from the tree. I was a teenager before I realized they were talking about a doe. Very few doe permits were issued. If one was shot, it had to remain in the woodshed until it was butchered.

Jude and I always sat on the bench next to the wall with our backs to the windows. We couldn't enjoy our turkey dinner if we sat facing that maple tree where the dead bucks hung. Mom got up early and fixed the Thanksgiving meal. How she managed to cook everything on a woodstove is beyond me, but the turkey was always done to perfection. Apple, pumpkin, and mincemeat pies had been baked the day before and were stored in the pantry where it was cool enough to keep them fresh without actually freezing them. Along with the usual fare, our dinner wasn't complete without red Jell-O on a lettuce leaf. Nobody ate it, of course, but it looked pretty. Once the meal was consumed, Dad rested for less than an hour before he rejoined the relatives who had gone to their own homes for the Thanksgiving meal. The men were ready to hunt until dusk. Jude and I helped Mom wash the dishes and put away the leftovers. The turkey remained on a platter and was covered with tin foil, but we didn't put it in the fridge. It was kept on the pantry table where it was within easy reach for an evening snack. It would be unthinkable to store turkey in a cold pantry today, but that's the way we did it many years ago.

C'mon, the Snow is Packy

Those few words signaled a winter afternoon of rolling tiny snowballs into three large rounds resulting in the perfect four-foot snowman. In the old days, no youngster could resist the fun involved in such a project. Even house cats like me reached for our warmest clothes and ran outside to help with the rolling. It had to be done with exact precision or the bottom round would throw Frosty off center. Nobody wanted a tipsy snowman. He was proof positive that the wannabe structural engineers had a long way to go before they were experts.

Because Jude was the oldest, she initiated the rolling and made sure we didn't go only in one direction. In order to maintain a circular pattern, rolling to the left and right was mandatory. It didn't matter if Pepper, Waggs, or Sparky had yellowed the snow. Once they had relieved themselves, the dogs got out of our way as we rolled around the front yard.

Packy snow is full of moisture. Sometimes it was too heavy for one person to roll. In that case, Ed and I stopped working on the belly and head and assisted Jude. Six hands pushed and shoved until our leader commanded us to halt. The first round was big enough—not because Jude said so but because it refused to roll any farther. Where it stopped was where it stayed even if it was a bit lumpy. Then we started making the belly and head. With great ceremony, one was hoisted on top of the other. Then we stood back and admired our creation.

If Frosty needed a little adjusting, our sister made the necessary modifications. Perhaps another handful of snow was added to the belly or packed around the middle to ensure stability. If the head appeared too small or too large, snow was pinched off or added. Prior to building our snowman, we had taken a carrot from the refrigerator, snatched one of Dad's caps, and grabbed a scarf with holes in it. Then we dug in the coal pail for small pieces that would become the eyes and mouth. Larger pieces were the buttons. Twigs were bountiful but not always perfect. It wasn't unusual for Frosty to have one arm longer than the other. One hand might have fingers while the other lacked both and stuck straight out. Sometimes the carrot nose remained where it belonged. Other times it refused to stay lodged, fell to the ground, and was quickly claimed by one of the dogs.

Packy snow didn't last long. It was crucial to make a snowman family before fluffy snow fell and ruined our chances. Sometimes there wasn't much snow and our yard was patchy, which meant blades of grass or weeds were rolled with the snow that created Frosty's wife and kid. After we wrapped a bandana around Mrs. Frosty's head, we fancied her up with leaf earrings. Then we put mittens on the kid's stick hands and our outdoor fun was over. We were ready for the hot chocolate Mom had waiting for us. As we drank it, our mittens and snowpants dried on the Jungers. We lay on the floor, warmed our stocking feet on the stove, and planned our next project when the snow, once again, was packy and we were ready to roll.

Waiting for Christmas Catalogs

In the old days, long before the Internet, online shopping, credit cards, letters to Santa, and parents purchasing a $1000 worth of toys, kids looked forward to the Christmas catalogs. The anticipation was almost unbearable as we waited and watched for the catalogs to appear in the stores. When we were a little older, we checked the mailbox for the brown wrapper covering the gigantic book we knew would contain beautiful toys.

What a joy it was when Mom handed us the catalog and it was finally our turn to thumb through the pages. Nobody cared about clothes or gave a moment's thought to the latest styles. We wanted to see what the newest toys were. For Jude it might have been a set of Chinese checkers or some other board game. Ed would have searched for plastic cowboys, soldiers, or metal dump trucks. I was only interested in dolls and all the stuff that went with them. If we had spent as much time in the World Book Encyclopedia as we spent in those catalogs, we would have been scholars. Within two weeks, pages were dog-eared and toys were circled then crossed out when something better caught our eye. Item descriptions and page numbers were memorized. If anyone dared tear out a page and hide it, the hunt was on to find it. Squabbles ensued with accusations flying left and right.

We loved everything about those catalogs. From the smell to the slippery pages to the colorful descriptions of each and every toy, our fascination never wavered. No matter how many times we looked at our favorite items, we never tired of repeatedly examining them in case we had missed something the first thirty-five times we had checked them out. After we got home from school, changed into our old clothes, did our chores and homework, ate supper and washed up before going to bed, we sat at the kitchen table and pored over the pages that had become as familiar to us as our names.

We had a two-dollar limit. That's why it was imperative to re-examine our choices. We had to get the best bang for our bucks. If one toy cost a quarter, another was forty-five cents and a third was a dollar, we would pick out something else to get to the two dollar maximum even it if meant changing our original purchases. It would have been unthinkable not to spend all we were allotted.

What we didn't know until Christmas morning was that Mom had been keeping a sharp eye on something we coveted the most but couldn't afford. "Santa" usually brought the gift we desired but lacked the funds to purchase. The surprise and sheer delight of finding that special toy underneath the tree was like heaven. We didn't know then what we know now: Parents want to give their children everything they ask for but realize one special, unexpected gift will tell them how much they are loved. No need to spend a fortune on a mountain of junk.

An Evening in Paris

The only cologne I recall Mom wearing was Evening in Paris, a yearly Christmas gift from us kids. There was something mysteriously wonderful about that chic blue bottle of scent that lent an aura of sophistication to Mom. She was transformed from a farmer's wife in patched barn overalls to a refined lady. Such was the effect of the much-loved fragrance of "Paris."

In the 1950s, it was common for children to amuse themselves without the aid of electronic gizmos. One of my favorite games was playing "dress up." I had a collection of old dresses, hats, gloves, and high heels that were put to good use. I spent hours in my playhouse pretending I was a wealthy lady who traveled from one exotic place to another. One evening I visited Paris. It was only natural I would purchase a bottle of cologne bearing the same name.

It's amazing what images a fancy blue bottle can conjure. The magic of a few drops of cologne dabbed on my wrists transported me from our farm to a city I still haven't seen and probably never will. But as a girl, Paris was the destination I longed to visit and see the Eiffel Tower and walk the streets of Madame Defarge. Although she was an unsavory character created by Dickens, she lived in the glorious "City of Lights," the place I wanted to be.

Ah, sweet youth. You gave us freedom from the cares of adulthood. For a few short years, we were oblivious to everything outside our immediate realm. Our childhood kingdom was filled with opportunities. We didn't realize they were mostly unobtainable. We only knew our imagination was the most magnificent playmate we had. Girls could be Nancy Drew, Annie Oakley, Jo from *Little Women* or any other girl we read about. Boys could be Roy Rogers, Gene Autry, Wild Bill Hickok, or a brave soldier on the battlefield. We created our own reality where we lived for a short while until our mother reminded us it was chore or suppertime. Then we temporarily left our enchanting world of make-believe.

Gone are the days of creative play ungoverned by colorful dots on a screen. Perhaps the hand/eye coordination of children in this century is enhanced by electronics. Perhaps technology will make them more likely to succeed in our modern world. I don't know, but I remember what fun it was dressing up in Mom's discarded outfits and high heels and being whisked away to the magical city of Paris if only in my mind.

My Red Wool Dress

When I was fifteen, I was invited to a wedding. The event required attire fancier than a skirt and blouse. Such clothing was appropriate for school, but not for such a special occasion. Mom and I scoured the shops on Ashmun Street in Sault Ste. Marie. A long time ago, our downtown was lined with a variety of clothing shops as well as the usual department stores.

Although she was the wife of a farmer and the daughter of one, Mom had an innate sense of style she imparted to me at an early age. Anyone who knows me now is aware I'm the least stylish person in Michigan. However, I didn't always dress like a bum. There was a time when I was quite fashionable, or at least I thought so. Anyway, while searching for the perfect dress Mom and I walked up one side of the street and down the other. I was ready to give up when she spied a red wool beauty with a black belt. It was the right length and a wonderful color for a December wedding, but I had one major concern. The dress had short sleeves. Although it was winter, it wasn't the lack of long sleeves that bothered me. It was the hair on my arms.

In those days the hair on my arms and legs grew faster than weeds in a vegetable garden. Whatever I was eating must have acted as potent fertilizer. I was never permitted to use a razor because Mom was worried I might slice off a chunk of my kneecap or ankle. Some gals will remember those wonderful sandpaper sleeves our mothers purchased to minimize a shaving accident. They worked great in removing hair and even better in giving burns. With the hayfield of hair on my legs, it was necessary to rub hard, which resulted in smooth, hairless legs with no nicks, only sandpaper burns. So as I stood in front of the shop's dressing room mirror, I didn't see the pretty red dress. All I saw were my hairy arms. Mom was getting impatient and asked what was taking so long. Did I need help with the zipper? No, I didn't need zipper assistance. My dilemma was much more serious than that.

I finally plucked up courage and emerged. Mom said the dress was lovely and a perfect fit. We would take it. I agreed, because in those days teenagers didn't argue with their mother if they were lucky enough to get a new garment. When the wedding day arrived, I wore that red wool dress with the short sleeves and thin black belt. Nobody paid me the slightest bit of attention. People were too busy wondering if the bride "had" to get married and if the groom was drunk or just acting silly when he slurred "till death do us part."

Once the nuptials were out of the way, it was on to the hall, the dinner and the dance. I forgot all about my arms when the most attractive guy in the wedding party waltzed me across the room. I wore that dress many times after the initial outing and never once did I give my hairy arms a second thought. Vanity had fled without a word of farewell, replaced by a dose of self-confidence imparted by a handsome young dance partner.

The Seasons of 1957

Growing up in the 1950s was a lot different than it is today. In those days, the county lacked the sophisticated equipment required to level snow banks. As kids, we dug holes in the four-feet-high banks and hollowed out forts. We stockpiled snowballs and created our own wireless amusement by having snowball fights. Only a handful of kids lived on our road and most of us were related, so our fights were friendly if fierce.

When the gravel road was icy, it wasn't uncommon to lace up ice skates and practice skating on the road. We never worried about cars because there were none. The people to the left of us usually took M-28, and the two families to our right went out Six Mile Road. Obviously, Dad wasn't going to run over us when he came home from work so we didn't give a collision with an automobile a second thought.

April was a challenge for kids and cars. If the frost left slowly, which meant freezing at night and melting a little during the day, our car could usually make it to the corner without getting stuck. However, if the frost left fast, the road became a muddy, mucky mess. Often the county put up a "Road Closed" sign at either end. The school bus wouldn't venture down our road because the driver knew he'd never make it through. There was only one way to catch the bus and that was to walk to Six Mile, or the Old Brimley Road as it was then called. It was a one-mile walk, but in the early morning I don't recall anyone grumbling. We all sojourned together, heedless of the brisk air and deep ruts. If it had been a mild night, our boots were covered with mud. Often it would suck off a boot, and we walked out of it. When this happened, the boot stayed behind while our foot kept going. Many a time I walked out of my boot and had to lean on someone while another kid pulled my boot out of the mud. Then I wiped off my shoe, slipped the boot back on, and we continued on our way.

Sometimes one of our parents picked us up after school or met the bus at the corner. Nobody owned a good car in those days. The driver plowed through the mud, and we held on to the seat in front of us. There was no such thing as a seat belt. Our ride was a harrowing one, but we always made it home safe and sound. The county paved a stretch of my road in 1998. All the new folks living here have no idea what it was like to drive through squishy, sloppy mud.

In the summer, we rode our bicycles on gravel. It probably took me two summers before I mastered a two-wheeler. "Training wheels" were unheard of. We trained ourselves by continuously falling until we learned to balance long enough to stay upright. Falling on sharp stones was no picnic. Skinned elbows and knees were the norm. Forget about helmets. If they had been available and anyone had worn one, we would have considered him an alien from another planet or a sissy from the Soo.

The prettiest time of year was autumn. Our woods were ablaze with color. The silent fields had yielded their crops of oats or hay, and the pastures rested from the tramp of cattle. When cold October winds blew into November, our milk cows stayed in the barn where the heat from their bodies lent warmth to the building. As the months passed, calves were born and nourished by their mothers. They stayed together and got acquainted. Once weaned, the calves were moved to their own stalls and drank warm milk from a pail instead of the natural source.

Our barn was originally a log cabin. Over the years, previous owners had built a house and the cabin went to the cows. Our horse barn and chicken coop were later additions. A haymow was constructed, a metal roof nailed in place and our barn became a welcome home for the animals. The few times I ventured to their domain, I loved the smell of hay and freshly cleaned stalls. There was a feeling of peace and contentment in the simple wooden structures that couldn't be matched by the cement floor and metal stanchions of my uncle's barn.

Although all the seasons were magical, April was and still remains my favorite month. After a long, hard winter, April gives us the promise that things will get better. The sun stays around longer and shines brighter. Daffodils, crocus, and other hardy perennials brave the solid ground and make their way to the surface. Robins return to build their nests in the arms of their favorite trees. Rivers overflow their banks. Kids put away their sleds and get out their bicycles. The countdown to the end of the school year begins. As youngsters, we waited for the return of summer when our road would once again come alive with the echo of bicycles on gravel, wooden bats hitting home runs, and innocent voices calling us to come out and play.

Waiting on Belle

This story is about the night Belle freshened. It was the first time I was allowed to witness a birth. All day I had begged Mom to let me watch. First she said no, but I pestered until she finally gave in. I felt sorry for Belle because she was unlucky. Something was always wrong with her calf and Dad had to shoot it. According to an entry in my 1959 diary, I prayed all that day and had a feeling this calf would be normal.

Earlier in the afternoon, Dad had called the vet. Belle had been in labor for a long time. The vet didn't hold out much hope for either Belle or her calf. He said the birth would be breech. He told Dad to have his rifle ready in case things went wrong. Dad told him to go home. He said he'd let nature take its course and not hurry the shooting if it had to be done.

Dusk was descending when Mom told me to go back to the house, but I didn't. I stood outside the barn and imagined what thoughts were passing through Belle's mind. Words came to me as clearly as if she had put them in my ears. I imagined her thinking that she didn't know where the pain ended and her calf began. I was only twelve and didn't know anything about the birthing process, but I thought there must come a point when there's no difference between the pain of being born and the pain of dying.

Dad opened the barn door and broke into my thoughts. He said he knew I hadn't gone to the house. He came out to make sure I was okay. He lit a Camel. The smell of lighter fluid and puffs of smoke filled the air. He pointed out the Big Dipper but said he didn't know the names of the other constellations. I knew his schooling ended in the third grade when winter came and his feet could no longer bear the cold ground as he walked to school. When his Pa died a year later, Dad inherited the only thing of value—a prized pair of black boots with no patches. Gram lost the farm that spring and moved Dad and his sisters from place to place. Eventually they homesteaded the twenty acres on a sideroad five miles east of Brimley. It's where I live now.

Dad and I returned to the barn and Mom said it was okay if I stayed a little longer. I sat on a bale of hay next to Gram. She held my hand. Mom rested her head on Dad's shoulder. I remember thinking that if love could be measured by touch or glance or motion, it would still have remained measureless in our barn that night.

My thoughts again turned to what might be going through Belle's mind. I was always making up stories. Like Gram, I liked to read. Maybe it was all the words floating in my head or maybe it was just my imagination, but I always thought animals were smarter than humans because they were obedient. As a Catholic, I knew obedience was the most important virtue. Cows were obedient because they walked up the ramp of Dunbar's truck when he came to our place and picked up the animals that were headed for auction. Maybe they knew they were going to their death. Maybe not, but it always made me sad when I saw that truck drive down our lane.

I heard Dad say it was time. He called to Mom and Gram. They reassured and encouraged him to have faith. Mom told me to turn away, and I did. I didn't see the calf being born but Dad cheered because it came out the right way. I saw it wobble to its feet. It was a healthy little heifer. I watched Belle lick her baby, and I cried tears of thankfulness right along with Mom and Gram. When Dad was certain all was well, he turned off the light, and we stepped into the night. The walk to the house was joyful.

The fire had burned low in the kitchen stove and although the room was cold, we didn't feel it. After hanging our barn jackets in the back shed and taking off our boots, Dad stirred the coals to life, got a flame going and added dry wood. It wasn't long before the chill left the kitchen. Mom made hot chocolate for me and tea for Gram and Dad. She set out a plate of sugar cookies Gram had baked earlier in the day.

We sat around the table and talked. That was the first and only time I was in the barn when a calf was born. Dad said it was no place for a young lady. He was a good man. Like others of his generation, he struggled to understand his role as husband and father. Because he brought his wife home to his mother, he was often caught between two strong-willed women, but that night there was no bickering, only the peace that comes after a long and weary battle.

Where Does Time Go?

Everybody wants to know where time goes. Most of us have no idea what happened to January, but we all know that after Valentine's Day, February will go just as fast. Once the fuss of St. Patrick's Day is over, March will gallop away with the last of winter's strong winds. April will disappear after Easter and then it's only a short hop to Mother's Day followed by Memorial Day. Soon thereafter we'll start looking for a gift for Dad. Waving the flag on the Fourth of July will follow in the blink of an eye.

I'll admit the passage of time doesn't go quite as fast as the five seconds it took to jump from January to July, but we all know time flies. At eleven years old, I began keeping track of time when I received a Timex wristwatch for Christmas. By today's standards, a pre-teen receiving her first watch at that ripe age is tantamount to child abuse, but in 1958 the gift was a treasure because it represented a grownup present.

In those days my eyes were good, so I had no problem reading the teeny weenie numbers, or watching the itty bitty hand sweep away the minutes. At school, I wouldn't have to sneak a peek at the clock and endure my teacher's scowl or listen to her tell me I should be concentrating on scholarly tasks instead of waiting for the day to end. I was sure the less fortunate kids would envy my present and probably want to wear it for an hour. The pleasure of gazing at that watch was most likely equivalent to today's kids looking at a $900 smart phone.

Jude had received a beautiful gold-tone Bulova wristwatch. For a fleeting moment I was jealous of my sister. Then my common sense kicked in, and I figured since she was in high school and I was in the sixth grade, it was only natural she should get the better watch. At least that's what I told myself. How much I believed it, I really don't know, but I know how the rest of that Christmas vacation went. According to entries in my diary, I walked around the house asking if anyone wanted to know the time. Nobody did, but that didn't slow me down. I told my sister, brother, parents, grandmother, and even the dogs what time it was, and I told them every few minutes. This went on until the end of vacation, by which time nobody was talking to me. Not even the dogs wanted to stay in any room I occupied.

On New Year's Day, I wrote that I was exhausted. For the first time in my life I must have realized how tiring it was to watch time, to be aware of the passing of every minute of every hour. It was one thing to wish for the end of a school day, but quite another to watch the hands of my little watch go about their business. Also, the stretchy silver band that looked so pretty in the box kept pinching me as the links caught the hair around my wrist. I didn't want to admit it, but time and I were on the outs.

Well anyway, enough of recalling time's past. Back to the present. After the Fourth of July, August gardens will produce their bounty, giving us time to can our beets, pickles, and zucchini relish to show at the county fair. A few days later, the yellow monsters of September will roar down quiet country roads picking up kids excited or horrified at the prospect of another school year. As October rain pelts little goblins, witches and Ninjas, we'll wish we hadn't eaten all the Snickers bars. Come November, we'll be planning the Thanksgiving feast and wondering if we should invite the relative nobody likes. What's left after the mad dash to Black Friday and Cyber Monday sales? Why, December and Christmas, of course. And there you have it. Another year gone before we know it and everybody asking where the time went.

There's Nothing Like a Good Scare

Sixty-five years ago, my sister decided to give me a good scare. Jude and I didn't have much in common. She loved the barn and I was a housecat. She loved Elvis. I liked Faron Young. I read books. Jude subscribed to motion picture magazines. I played with dolls endlessly while she concentrated on board games, outdoor activities, and sleeping. Jude loved to sleep. It wasn't unusual for her to be in bed when I was dressed and waiting for the school bus.

In those days, I could sit on the arm of the couch in the far front room and watch for the bus. No trees obscured my view so I could see the bus when it turned the corner about a half-mile away. That gave Jude just enough time to throw on some clothes, grab her lunch, and run down our lane. She was easygoing and always laughed at my seriousness. She saw no reason to give up an hour's sleep when she could easily get ready in five minutes.

When I was very young, Mom braided my hair and tied ribbons around the rubber bands. Jude's hair was a thick tangled mess held in place by barrettes. I scrubbed my neck and elbows every morning. Jude splashed water on her face and hands. My clothes were meticulously pressed as were Jude's, but it was her habit to grab whatever garment was at hand whether it was yesterday's dress or an outfit headed for the wash.

Every night before I went to bed, I stacked my books in a neat pile so they would be ready for the next day. Jude hunted for her stuff. My shoes were polished. Hers were scuffed. She saw the funny side of everything, while I saw only gloom. If we hadn't had the same parents, no one would have taken us for sisters.

Jude feared nothing, neither man nor beast, while I feared everything. She knew I was a fraidy cat and took full advantage of my timid nature. It wasn't unusual for her to hide behind a tree or a door and jump out and scare me. She wasn't mean. She was merely entertaining herself much the same as when we threw snowballs at our neighbor's ram, knowing full well it couldn't get through the fence.

One night, Jude hid in our bedroom and waited. She knew I would be along shortly. We had been to the drive-in and watched *Frankenstein*, a movie that terrified me because it seemed so real. As I reached to pull the string to the overhead light, Jude's icy cold hand grabbed my arm. I shrieked when she squeezed it. She didn't say a word as she slowly released her grip.

I pulled the light string, afraid I might see a monster. What I saw was Jude wearing a Halloween mask and reaching her hands towards me. I screamed. She howled with laughter. I started to cry. She removed the mask and said she didn't mean to scare me that bad. She was just having fun. Her hand was cold because she had soaked it in ice water. Then, uncharacteristically, she hugged me. It took me a long time to forget Frankenstein, but I never forgot Jude's hug.

From then on, we more or less came to an understanding. For the first time ever, she admitted that maybe it wasn't such a good idea to scare me in case I had a heart attack. It wouldn't look too good if she scared me to death. It would be hard to explain how a simple "BOO" had killed her sister. She said some of my habits bugged her because she thought I was perfect. I was surprised because I thought she was perfect. She had lots of friends and was never lonely while I had no friends and was alone all the time. I wanted to be like her and laugh at everything, but I didn't know how.

Jude passed away eight years ago. It was a quiet, unexpected death. She had called her grandson and asked him to pick up something from Walmart. About thirty minutes later, Steven opened her bedroom door and found her in that deep sleep from which there is no awaking. She had slipped away without a word to anyone. She was a widow and lived alone, so no one was with her when she left this world. But knowing Jude, I could almost hear her say with a chuckle in her voice, "Don't be afraid, Sharon. Why, there's nothing to it. Just close your eyes, release your spirit, and God will welcome you home."

Part II:
Celebrating
the Holidays

The Folly of New Year's Resolutions

If you're still feeling as stuffed as the Christmas goose, it's time to talk turkey. Most women in my age bracket gain weight whether we eat a carrot or a seven-course meal. It's just an unalterable fact of growing older. Sure, I know there are some lucky gals who remain slim and trim throughout their lives, but they're in the minority. So chin up, ladies, we're all in this kettle of fish together. I keep thinking I'm forty years younger than I am. I don't feel old. I don't dress in polyester pantsuits. I don't have blue hair. I don't wear housedresses or bib aprons like Mom did. I don't own a purse that snaps when I close it. There is no fur encircling the top of my snowboots or the collar of my winter coat. I don't have a bridge, an implant, or a set of choppers other than my own. I don't feel old until I pass by a mirror.

Most of us threw out our full-length mirrors when things started heading south. Now we take a quick glance in the bathroom mirror when we comb our hair or put on some makeup in hopes it will cover an assortment of colorful spots that appear out of nowhere. Makeup does little to hide them, but making the attempt boosts our morale. We pluck a few wayward white eyebrows and maybe even a few pesky hairs sprouting from you know where. We dab on a little rouge, run a powder puff over our face, and get out the magnifying glass to find our lips.

Before we leave the house, we take one final look. The mirror tells us we're presentable because we only see our face. The rest of our person is hidden from view and that's nothing short of a blessing. For those of us who were always thin, seeing our hips spreading across our frame like butter spreading across a slice of warm toast is enough to discourage us from taking one step beyond our own threshold. It isn't vanity that makes us cringe at our appearance and yearn for the good old days of our youth. It's something entirely different. It's a feeling of total and complete hopelessness.

It's a terrible thing to lose hope. Without it, we are forced to face the inevitable. We will never again be thin. We'll never squeeze into anything smaller than a size 1X. We must be willing to accept what we cannot change. I do not care what all the ads say about weight loss. Once we hit a certain age, it's a losing battle and we might as well admit it. We must train ourselves to look past the chocolate cake sitting on the counter and begging us to eat the last slice. We must leave the pistachios and mints in the candy dish. We must make a firm decision to honor the resolution we made on January 1.

Never again will we order a strawberry shake from McDonald's because never again will we stop at a fast food restaurant. The tasty thin crust pizza we were so fond of will go the way of the milkshake. We don't care when the Dairy Queen opens in the spring, because a hot fudge sundae is a treat of the past. For the remainder of our lives, we're doomed to a plate of uninspiring greens wilting before our eyes. We'll devour radishes by the pound and celery stalks by the dozen. We'll crunch our way through bowls of broccoli, cauliflower, and popcorn as dry as kindling.

But wait a minute. Is it really so bad to be old and gain weight just thinking about food? Any kind of food. It doesn't have to be crammed full of calories. I put on weight merely by drinking water. If the plain liquid from the tap in my kitchen has become my enemy, what chance do I have when it comes to eating a meal, even one made of quinoa and green beans? None, that's what. No chance whatsoever. So why am I concerned about my appearance? Why am I worried what folks will say about my new exterior? Could it be that my old foe, vanity, is still alive within me? Maybe it isn't hopelessness at all. Maybe the obsession with my looks all boils down to vanity. What if people start praising my great personality? That would be worse than saying I'm hefty. Being known for my personality would be humiliating. I was never known for my personality. I don't even know if I have one.

Maybe my wit will save me. I can be a clever old gal without even trying, but sometimes my cleverness might lean a little toward sarcasm if the listener doesn't have a sense of humor. While writing this column, I gave myself a serious talk. The more I thought about things, the less concerned I was about the extra pounds that crept up on me while I was sleeping. I was more concerned about my sharp tongue. When you've lived alone as long as I have, you tend to forget you're talking to someone other than yourself. But be that as it may, gather around, ladies. If you, too, mourn the loss of your girlish figure, try to remember all you haven't lost. At the Thanksgiving and Christmas tables, nobody noticed your weight. They praised the food and thanked God the family was together. A glass was raised to you, the cook.

In that moment, you knew you were loved beyond measure. Loved beyond what the scales said. Loved because of who you are not what size you are. So, forget that resolution wherein you promised yourself you would lose thirty pounds in thirty days. Lose what you can, stay healthy, and know I'm cheering you on as I toast the New Year in with the last of the Evan Williams spiked eggnog.

The Hope and Dismay of Valentine's Day

Well, here we are in the shortest month of the year. February will gallop by as fast as a thoroughbred runs for the roses. There's not much point in bemoaning the speed at which time passes because there's not one thing we can do about it. We often hear philosophers and preachers telling us to live each day as if it were our last. We know that's impossible. Most of us could manage a few days, maybe even an entire week, but to live every day as a loving, kind, patient, thoughtful human being would drive us to drink if it didn't drive us nuts first.

The greatest event in February is a day all females look forward to as eagerly as Cupid. Women of all ages anticipate Valentine's Day for the wonderful surprises it brings. It's the perfect day for fellows to pop the question and end their carefree bachelor life. If they can't muster the courage to permanently shackle themselves to their lady love, they can send her a beautiful heart-shaped box of candy or a bouquet of yellow roses symbolizing friendship. But here's a warning to all single chaps who might be reading this. Beware the beautiful red rose. In the eyes of your darling, a yellow rose is an automatic invitation for you to hit the road, but the red rose means wedding bells so choose your rose color wisely.

No Brimley boy ever permanently captured my affection, but none of them put forth much effort. Their valentines expressed what their heart might have felt but their mouth couldn't say. Or maybe the fellow's mother addressed the card, and the boy had no idea what he was giving. In the old days valentines came with white envelopes. It wasn't unusual for a kid to write his name on the back of each valentine while his parent wrote the name of the intended recipient on the front. Perhaps the boy asking me to be his valentine had no idea and wondered why I smiled at him so sweetly. Maybe he thought I was off my rocker. There was one young lad who won my heart at the tender age of seven. We sat at the same table in first grade. As the years passed and tables gave way to desks, this handsome chap sat behind me when we were placed in alphabetical order. Unless, of course, I landed in the last seat of the row. In that case, my admirer was in the first seat of the next row and that's where he stayed all year.

From that distance, he was unable to pull my hair or poke me with a pencil eraser, things little boys did to get a girl's attention. I suppose if a kid did that in today's schools, the boy would be banished to the principal's office where a policeman would haul him off to the jailhouse. The little girl would be whisked off to the counselor's office, asked to relive the terrifying experience, and spend the rest of her school years in a recovery program. But when I was young, children were unsophisticated. We didn't know it was traumatic to have a braid pulled or an elbow pushed while we wrote. If a boy did such things, it meant he liked the girl. I remember a boy who used to hit girls over the head with a book to show his affection. Nobody thought of it as an act of violence. We thought it was fun, stood in line, and awaited our turn to get our head banged.

Valentines for school children now often have themes reflecting popular movie or action heroes. Gone is the image of a little boy dressed as a cowboy throwing a lasso over his special girl. Gone, too, are valentines depicting boys in overalls and girls in pretty dresses. Years ago our valentines were as simple as we were. We didn't depend upon superheroes because they didn't exist unless you count Rin Tin Tin, the Lone Ranger, or Lassie.

Here's hoping your valentine remembers you on the on the fourteenth with candy, flowers, a pretty card, and a nice dinner. If he forgets this special day, give him a good poke with a pencil eraser. Such an act might beat him into submission, if not to the altar. That might take Cupid's bow and arrow, George Washington's hatchet, or a posthumous Proclamation from President Lincoln.

Forty Days and Forty Nights

The memories of my youth stir embers into flames when the season I dreaded most draws nigh. Another year, another forty days of fasting, another Lent. Oh, how I hated those days of my childhood. No bridge mix candy, no black licorice, not even a hint of Black Jack gum, and certainly no creamy Cadbury Caramello bars. My siblings and I looked forward to Lent about as much as a condemned man looks forward to the gallows.

The collecting of sweets began weeks prior to Ash Wednesday. We checked every cookie jar and box of Whitman's chocolates. We searched high and low for any candy that had previously escaped our notice. Even a Queen Anne's Chocolate Covered Cherry left over from Christmas would have passed our "Candy Worth Saving" test. As soldiers prepare for battle so we prepared for what was coming. Believe me, it was no easy task. If we were lucky enough to be given a Mounds bar, we consumed one section and hid the other. If handed a Bit-O-Honey, we broke off a couple pieces and hoarded the rest. A Sugar Daddy was given a few licks and wrapped up again. Dubble

Bubble was put aside as an emergency ration. Even the chocolate covered raisins picked out of the bridge mix looked appetizing after the first few weeks of fasting. We followed the rules as steadfastly as if our mother were standing guard over us every second of the minutes, every minute of the hours. The thought of cheating did not occur to us. It would have been unthinkable to break the fast and endure the humiliation heaped upon us by a sibling. I can almost hear Jude saying, "You couldn't last a week? A mere six days without sugar? You weakling."

For, you see, in our church, the forty days of fasting did not include Sundays. I have no idea how old I was when this wonderful loophole was discovered. I might have been ten before learning it was okay to devour some of my stash on Sunday. I loved licorice and would stuff myself with Black Licorice Wheels, Black Jack Taffy, or Red Anise Squares. When I started feeling sick, I'm sure I shared my hoard with my siblings.

When I was young, being Catholic was hard work. It wasn't the cakewalk it is today. In the old days, breaking rules and regulations could land us in hell. It wasn't our parents we feared. It was God. He was a tyrant looking for any excuse to beat us into submission. I was sure I'd be struck dead if I licked a Sugar Daddy on a Monday in Lent. Obviously, I must have followed the rules because I survived to tell this tale.

Continuation of the Lenten Season

Fear started on opening day when the priest ground ashes into my forehead, made the sign of the cross, and told me to remember that I was dust and unto dust I would return. Mom probably walked with us to the front of the church when we were very young, but by age seven we were on our own. I'm fairly certain I didn't want to think about death and dust. I wanted to play with my dolls and be happy, but that black cross was a reminder I'd better be good or I was headed for hell.

Hell was as much a part of my youth as was the Baltimore Catechism. Our priest arrived in Brimley when I was eight years old and departed ten years later. Throughout my childhood and teenage years, he and the catechism represented God, who was a hard taskmaster. Or maybe it was the teachings of our church that were harsh. With all the rules and regulations, it was a full-time job trying to avoid sin. When I was a youngster, sin was everywhere. It was in the last cookie I ate and blamed its disappearance on my sister. It was hidden in the piece of cake I fed to one of our dogs and told Mom I had eaten. It was baptizing my dolls and forgetting to say my prayers. My biggest sin was fear of God. He seemed like a hateful old man instead of a loving heavenly father. Life was a complicated, sinful mess for Catholic children. If a question couldn't be answered by our catechism as to why something was sinful, it was no problem. Our teacher told us to have faith, trust in God, and not get too nosy about things we didn't understand.

I remember something that happened during catechism class one Saturday morning in Lent. I have no idea what was being taught because I was distracted by a strange feeling on my neck. When I couldn't stand it any longer, I raised my hand and squished a spider, all the while feigning interest in the lesson. If a family of spiders had been spinning a web at the nape of my neck I would have kept quiet. Fear held my tongue. In the old days fear, sin, and punishment by way of hell fire were great motivators for silencing children.

Maybe that was a good thing, maybe not. I only know I was glad when Lent was over and the black cross forgotten. I made my Easter Duty and confessed my sins. The gravest ones might have landed me in hell. Those included ignoring my teachers, killing a spider, and finding and consuming a hidden chocolate bunny destined for my Easter basket.

Don't Forget to Wear Something Green

On St. Patrick's Day, Dad drilled into us kids the importance of wearing something green and proudly pinning a shamrock on our clothing. March 17 was the only day of the year orange was an absolutely forbidden color for it was a reminder of the old troubles between Catholics and Protestants. The animosity was so great, I remember Gram telling us the Catholic Church was burned to the ground in the dry town of Pickford, twenty miles south of Brimley. I have no idea if the story is true, so don't get your hackles up if it's as false as the set of teeth soaking in a glass on your nightstand.

Although most of the traditions of my youth have gone by the wayside, I continue to honor Dad's request. Even if I stay home and no one sees me, I'll wear something green on St. Patrick's Day. I did sell the shillelaghs I bought Dad when I lived downstate, and the last time I raised a glass of green stout was probably in 1977. The Old Shillelagh Pub in Detroit's Greektown was the place to be on St. Patrick's Day. Sometimes things got a little rowdy. I remember pouring a glass of beer down the front of a waitress's blouse. Do I recall the circumstances? Definitely, but the reason will go the way of the fellow I was with at the time and will never be told. My lips are sealed, and nine years ago George went to that great Irish tavern in the sky so you're not likely to hear a word from him.

In the office where I worked, girls who wouldn't be caught dead wearing anything green decked themselves out in various shades of clothing as bright as freshly cut sod. Even the most conservative lawyer wore a tie with a Celtic knot design or pinned a shamrock to his lapel. For one day, our sedate legal firm on the 21st floor of a downtown Detroit building became a place of merriment and goodwill. A senior partner would arrange a catered lunch of corned beef sandwiches and green sugar cookies. Once the workday ended, the mad dash to local drinking establishments was on. Along with Irish music, Guinness stout and Harp lager, Connemara whiskey poured forth like a river. With the aid of these beverages, there wasn't a dry throat or eye in the place by midnight. If anyone was still sober by the 18th, he had proven he was no Irishman and might as well fold his merino wool sweater, shove it back in a drawer, and try again next year.

George had never kissed the Blarney Stone, consumed Mulligan stew or tasted fresh soda bread baked in a traditional bastible, but none of that mattered. In the Old Shillelagh on St. Paddy's Day, he was more Irish than a leprechaun. Although he was a gifted illustrator, he had no musical ability, a minor detail we overlooked as he sang along to "Danny Boy" until tears rolled down his cheeks and his feigned brogue got as thick as his tongue. As the evening wore on and the crowd got rowdier, George marched in place to "A Nation Once Again" and mourned dear "Mother Machree." I must admit neither of us cared much for traditional Irish instruments or Celtic folk songs sung in the ancient language. We preferred the familiar Irish-American songs sung by performers like Pat's People and the Irish Rovers.

Along with wit, song and drink, the Irish have wonderful blessings. Here's one to remember as you go on your way: "May the road rise up to meet you. May the wind always be at your back. May the sun shine warm upon your face and the rain fall softly upon your fields. And until we meet again, may God hold you in the palm of His hand."

A Muddy April Road

Recently, I was going through old letters and found one Mom had written me about a Sunday in April 1979 when she and Dad were going to church. The frost was coming out of their road, but Dad figured it wouldn't be too sloppy on the way home if the sermon wasn't too long. Either the priest was particularly talkative that day or my parents stopped at Doran's Market, but the upshot was when they reached our road, they went down one hill but couldn't make it up the other. Getting stuck in the mud was nothing new. They pulled their boots from the back seat, put them over their shoes, and hoofed it a quarter-mile home.

My parents always dressed nice when they went to town or church. When I read Mom's letter, I envisioned her wearing her good coat with the fur collar. Her hat would have been a little black one with a dotted veil. Her black purse would have dangled from her elbow as she clutched Dad's arm. He would have worn his best jacket and gray fedora hat. They must have made quite a sight as they walked across the bridge and up the hill towards home. Only a handful of people lived on our road in those days. No one offered them a ride, and they probably wouldn't have accepted it anyway for fear their neighbor would also have gotten stuck. When they got home, they changed into their work clothes.

Mom said Dad got the tractor going, she perched upon the fender, and they started back down the road. Dad turned the tractor around and hitched a chain to the car. Mom sat behind the wheel and steered as best she could through the muddy ruts. It took a while, but eventually they made it to the driveway. Mom vowed she was not going out again until the road was free of frost. Her letters always ended on a cheerful note. She said God would understand if they missed Sunday mass. After all, she reasoned, He was the one who decided when the driving was good, and He could take the blame if the road was nothing but mud.

There's still one section of our road that isn't paved going towards M-28. Apparently, it's in a different township. When the county was paving our section in 1998, they quit at the second corner, but they did dig deep ditches that made a huge difference. So, although it's only gravel, it's nothing like it was in the old days. I drove out that way a couple weeks ago. My clean car was splattered with mud, but compared to years ago, it was smooth sailing.

Reading Mom's letters fifty years later transported me back to a time that is no more. Whether it was walking on a muddy road or helping Dad fix fences, her letters told the stories of her life when we were apart. Modern technology is great, but nothing beats holding a letter in my hand that was written by my dear departed Mother.

Waltzing with My Mother

When I was a youngster, the kitchen radio was always tuned to the only station we could get during the daytime, WSOO-AM. I remember trying to dance to the music of Hank Williams, Kitty Wells, Red Foley, and lots of other country singers. Whenever the mood overtook me, I would slide across the linoleum floor until my anklets were no longer bright white. My attempts at mimicking Ginger Rogers were pathetic, but that didn't dim my desire to dance.

One summer day Mom got tired of watching me whirl around the kitchen with an invisible partner. She decided it was time I learned the proper way to waltz so I would be ready if a fellow ever had the courage to invite me to a school dance when I was older. Most of the boys were afraid of me because I had a tendency to speak my mind, but no matter. You know what mothers are like. They have great faith in their children's prospects. Mom shook the flour from her hands, put a pie in the oven, and took off her apron. Then she took my hand.

She started with a basic step much like a square. Once I learned the simple concept of moving my feet in the right direction without looking at them, we advanced to more sophisticated steps. When she was fairly certain I wouldn't trip over my feet or get mine tangled up with hers, she suggested I take off my shoes. She said nobody could glide across the dance floor in a pair of clodhoppers. For the safety of her feet, neither of us had removed our shoes at the beginning of our lessons. By lesson five, she was pretty sure I wouldn't trample on her toes so off came the oxfords.

When the music started and Mom's arm was around me, I realized she was teaching me something I would love for the rest of my life. I have no idea what songs the DJ played as we slid across the floor. I only knew I never wanted to stop dancing. The heat from the woodstove didn't bother me. I ignored the jeers of my siblings. I tried my best to follow Mom's lead. My movements might have been a bit awkward, but she encouraged me whenever I took a wrong step. She knew nothing could hinder my determination to learn to waltz.

We didn't just slow dance. We didn't stand in one spot and sway to the music. I don't call that dancing. I have no idea how or when Mom learned to waltz, but she was an expert. Many times during that summer, she waltzed me around the kitchen when she heard a favorite song. Lots of them were sad ones like "It Wasn't God Who Made Honky Tonk Angels," "Your Cheatin' Heart," "Nobody's Darlin' but Mine," and many others, but there was no sign of sadness in her eyes. She loved country music so even if the songs brought memories, they must have been tender ones.

As time flew by, Mom taught me more intricate steps, and we danced more often. It was the summer of 1959. I was only twelve years old, but even at that young age I couldn't keep still when I heard a song I liked. Maybe I was trying to dance away my blues and keep loneliness at bay. I was alone much of the time with only my dolls and books for company. My sister was four years my senior and didn't share my interests.

As summer passed and September signaled the start of another school year, I don't remember dancing very often. Homework took precedence, Mom's chores increased, and the magic of summer was gone. Although the radio was always on, there wasn't much opportunity to waltz across the floor. In those days, there wasn't a radio in every room so only our kitchen had been our ballroom. With winter fast approaching, dancing seemed like a frivolous pursuit. There was wood to stack, hay bales to be put around the outside perimeter of the house, the ten-gallon milk can to be brought in and kept filled with water for household needs, and dozens more tasks to make ready for winter. That summer was one of the happiest of my childhood.

As a teenager, I occasionally took Mom's hand and asked her to dance with me, but by the 1960s much of the music we loved was replaced with a new generation of singers and a new genre of music. It was impossible to waltz to rock and roll, and Mom wasn't interested in doing the Twist, the Mashed Potato, or the Monster Mash. If a DJ played a song we remembered from the previous decade, all the lovely memories came rushing back. Mom held out her hand, but instead of her taking the lead, it was my turn.

The other evening "I Wish I Had Someone to Love Me" popped into my head. It's also called "The Prisoner's Song" and it's one we often danced to. I listened to it on YouTube and it brought back visions of the past. I saw myself in Mom's arms in the old house that is no more. I saw the brown radio that was always atop our refrigerator and Puff, our house cat, sleeping on a stack of wood by the stove. I saw Gram on her cot, smiling as she watched us dance across the floor. All the memories came back like a sweet spring rain watering a parched and barren land.

Only once in my adult life did I have a dance partner. He was George the Greek, who tried to keep me by his side long after my feelings for him had fled. We took lessons at a Detroit studio, but it was too late to salvage the relationship. That was forty-five years ago and I still have not found anyone willing to hold out his hand and ask me to dance. So I do what I did as a youngster. I dance with myself and cherish my invisible partner.

If your mother is still with you, treasure her. A piece of your heart will go with her when she's gone. On Mother's Day, hold her close and dance with her. She might not recognize you, but her spirit will know she's in the arms of someone who loved her when she was young and healthy and who still loves her now that her youth and memory are gone. If she's in a wheelchair or confined to a hospice bed, play her favorite song as you "lay your cool hand on her brow." You might not get another chance to show her how much you love her.

Remembering the Departed

With all the fuss given to an extra shopping day at Walmart, the true meaning of Memorial Day has changed over the years. Today, folks are eager to fire up the grill and invite family and friends to a backyard barbecue. It's another three-day holiday for workers, and it's filled with fun and frivolity. It's a time to enjoy good company and warm sunshine after a long, harsh winter.

But before the merriment begins, some families take time to honor their departed loved ones by placing flowers or a flag at the gravesites. Remembering the deceased is a nice tradition, but in our busy virtual world it's often difficult to maintain family rituals. This is especially true as older generations pass away, taking long-established customs with them.

Although our family had not lost anyone to war, a trip to the cemetery was our Memorial Day routine. Before the day was changed to reflect a three-day weekend, we went to the graveyard the Sunday prior to Memorial Day. The afternoon was spent visiting graves of relatives. I could hear the sadness in Mom's voice as she told her silent audience a year's worth of news. Even as a teenager, the yearly trip didn't mean much to me because I didn't know any of the deceased, and I wasn't all that interested.

Over the past sixty years, things have changed. Now, when I visit the cemetery, I'm well acquainted with those who have passed away. I've lost my paternal grandmother, parents, niece, sister, all my aunts and uncles, and a number of cousins. Gone are the days when the trip was merely an act of obedience and duty instead of a gesture of respect and affection.

Losing loved ones to natural causes or unexpected accidents is hard enough, but enduring the loss due to war must be nearly impossible. It's not just Flanders Field in Belgium or the many other American cemeteries dotted throughout various continents that carry the pall of death, it's all those unknown sites where combat victims fell. I was taught never to walk on a grave, but I wonder how many unmarked resting places people have trod upon without realizing where they were stepping.

Between Memorial Day and D-Day, a contemplative mood always settles on me. As I watch documentaries of the Normandy Invasion and all the soldiers who lost their lives that day, I can't help but reflect on our society in general. Those of us getting on in years must sometimes scratch our head and wonder what went wrong. We're the Baby Boomer generation. Many of us lived on farms. We lacked the conveniences of indoor plumbing, furnaces, modern cook stoves, telephones, television, designer clothes, and all the electronic gadgets that are part of today's world. We attended college and graduated with degrees our parents lacked. Jobs were plentiful and our future was bright. We looked forward to a better life than Mom and Dad because we were the biggest and best generation of all, or so we were told.

No one knew the 21st century would bring high unemployment, social unrest, abject poverty, and homeless families reminiscent of the 1930s. How did this happen? How did our country go from being the most prosperous on earth to a ghost of its former self? I don't know the answer. Maybe greed had something to do with it. Maybe stupidity. Maybe we can blame the government. Some say too much. Others say too little. The rich will say it's the fault of the poor who will argue the blame falls at the feet of the rich.

Life used to be simple when we had so little. Sometimes I marvel at how far we've come and how much we've lost. Now we have politicians instead of statesmen. We have every piece of technology known to man, yet we have no more idea how to relax and enjoy it than a frog knows how to jump out of a pot of hot water. Kids are chauffeured to various activities, becoming dependent upon external stimuli instead of their imagination. Stress, a word unheard of in my youth, runs rampant across all generations.

Recently I was speaking with an acquaintance and the conversation turned to wars. I expressed my opinion that outwardly they haven't accomplished much lately. I was immediately told wars are necessary because they're good for the economy. I agreed some folks do profit from war but asked if that was a good enough reason to continue them. When watching documentaries, I've yet to hear a dying soldier shout, "Long live the economy." Midst the noise of the battlefield, it's always the call for mother and home that echoes the loudest. My acquaintance had no response.

Hopefully, those who get rich from wars will share their bounty with the heroes—men and women who fought the enemy and unwittingly paved the way for entrepreneurs to safely enter foreign lands and accumulate great wealth from new enterprises. It's something to think about on Memorial Day.

Sunday Memories of Dad

When I was very young, Dad wasn't much of a church-goer. He worked shifts so sometimes he wasn't home, other times he wasn't interested in attending Sunday mass. We usually rode with Uncle Steve, Mom's bachelor brother, who lived across the road. When he wasn't available, Mom took the wheel. Although she didn't have a license, Dad knew she was a good driver. She could handle the tractor so he figured she could make it five miles to Brimley and back without wrecking the car.

When Uncle Steve left the Upper Peninsula to follow construction jobs, Dad took us to church when the roads were too treacherous for Mom's driving ability. Sometimes he had just gotten home from the midnight shift and was tired. I remember Mom poking him when he nodded off during the sermon. We always sat in the pew second from the back. The church was full, so nobody knew Dad was asleep except maybe the people behind us unless they were sleeping, too. If men drank a little too much on Saturday night, church was a great place to catch a few winks before beginning the day's chores. I don't think Dad snored, at least not very loudly. Like the sleeping drunks around him, he wasn't bothering anyone.

There were two readings in our church. The first was from the epistles and the second from the gospels. The readings were nice, but I don't recall being inspired by the homily that followed, because our priest was rather temperamental. Instead of reflecting on the readings, he usually yelled about something that had riled him. Not enough money in the collection basket was a favorite topic, as was the indifference people showed to the imposed winter fuel offering so there wasn't much to miss regarding an uplifting sermon. Sometimes

I'm sure I felt like sleeping, too, but the noise coming from the man of the cloth pounding the pulpit was enough to keep me afraid and fully awake no matter how tired I might have been.

When church finally got out, we kids hounded Dad to get us ice cream cones at McCready's store west of Brimley. A dime bought a cone with two large scoops. We rarely stopped at a small establishment Dad called Horsefeather's. I don't know if that was the name of the people who owned it, or just Dad's nickname for it. Anyway, he wasn't bothered if we dripped ice cream on the car seats, but Mom didn't want chocolate staining our church clothes. In those days, girls wore pretty dresses and boys wore good trousers and white shirts. Even at a young age, I loved hats and gloves. Every Sunday morning Mom decked me out like a Christmas tree.

When the weeks before Father's Day rolled around, we usually had no idea what to get Dad. He didn't fish, trap, bowl, or barbecue. He did enjoy playing poker, but he already had enough cards to start his own business because he received a new deck every special occasion. As we got older, we scrounged the tourist shops on Portage Avenue for novelty cards. Some were tiny, others extra large. Some decks were fancy with interesting or exotic backs, but the only cards Dad used were plain old Bicycle ones from the dimestore.

I was about nine years old when Mom gave Dad a can of orange paint for Father's Day. When he unwrapped it, I thought it was the most ridiculous present of all time. Who would want paint and how could it possibly compare to a nice deck of cards? What I didn't know was the renegade relatives who occasionally invaded our garage had worn Dad's patience thin, and Mom decided it was time for action.

I had no idea when people stopped by for a visit, they wanted to borrow something. It was nothing big, maybe a hammer or saw, a special wrench or an axe. Dad always obliged, knowing full well he would never see his tool again. However, once he got that paint the story changed. Everything in the garage that wasn't nailed down got a slap of orange. From then on, when Dad returned the visit, he moseyed to the relative's garage. Whenever he spied an orange tool, he wrestled it from the offender and brought it home. He knew it would disappear again, but he wasn't worried. He had a full can of bright orange paint and plenty of brushes to guarantee a tool's return.

Eventually he pulled the plug on cards and suggested a new flashlight might be just the ticket if we wanted to get him something special. Over the years, flashlights accumulated like flies around a fresh cow pie. The flashlight phase was followed by the decade of maps. Dad was no traveler, but he loved maps. In 1968 my brother volunteered for the Army and went to Vietnam. I married and moved to Colorado. Between the two of us, Dad received enough maps to wallpaper the kitchen wall.

By the time he retired, our milk cows were long gone and eventually Dad sold the Herefords. Since there were no more barn chores, he finally had time for a hobby. His interest turned to puzzles. He enjoyed a challenge and had a gift for figuring out what went where. We gave him lots of three-dimensional puzzles, but his favorite ones were jigsaws. Five hundred pieces were put together in a snap, but a thousand pieces took him a little longer. A thoughtful nephew, Jim, bought him a two-sided puzzle that would have driven anyone other than Dad crazy. I don't know how long it took him, but when that puzzle was finished Mom framed it and hung it on the wall.

Once retired, Dad never missed church on Sunday and if my memory is correct, Mom no longer had to poke him awake during mass. And to this day I still find a hammer or screwdriver with a dab of orange on the handle, a reminder that although he is gone, his fondness for irritating our relatives is an amusing memory that always makes me smile.

We lost Dad in September of 1983. His passing was sudden, and we weren't prepared for it, but I have fond memories of Sunday mornings when he sat behind the wheel and honked the horn telling us to get a move on or we'd be late for church. It was a short drive, but we always arrived at least twenty minutes before the service began so he could catch a few winks prior to all the standing and kneeling our church demanded.

The Official Arrival of Summer

My calendar tells me today is the first day of summer. It's been a long time coming to the eastern end of the Upper Peninsula. With temperatures dipping to thirty then rising to eighty within a few hours, most residents wondered if summer would ever get here and stick around longer than fifty minutes. Today we're breathing a collective sigh of relief. If our calendars and smart phones tell us today is the official beginning of the new season, it must be true. Bathing suit time, gals. Get out your suntan lotion and head for the beach.

Everyone talks about how grand it is to live in the U.P. Books abound about the glorious scenery, abundance of wildlife, magnificent waterfalls, beautiful snowmobile and hiking trails, and vast vistas of pristine nature. Facebook is filled with posts written by people who would give "anything" to live in our little corner of the universe. They imagine our surroundings as a wilderness wonderland. A paradise where deer and bear roam as freely as the buffalo once did on the Great Plains. Folks below the Mighty Mackinac Bridge yearn for a cabin in the woods or near the shoreline of Lake Superior. They envision watching the sun set as they stroll hand-in-hand with their lover along a sandy beach.

And now that summer has finally arrived, it's time to welcome all those folks eager to join us for a week or two or even through the end of August. They'll get to experience the bliss we're all familiar with: Mosquitoes, ticks, horse flies, deer flies, icy cold lakes, roads closed for repair, seagulls making deposits on car hoods, beach closures due to various strains of bacteria, and a myriad of other things known only to those of us who call the U.P. our permanent home. But, no matter. Open the floodgates and let the tourists in.

In 1984, I returned to stay and was immediately smitten with the beauty of our area, especially the lakes and sky. I hadn't seen clouds in many years and thought they were spectacular. Snow left early during my first winter here. No more than a few flakes fell after Valentine's Day. I told Mom things sure had changed and said there was more snow in Detroit than in Brimley. She laughed and told me to stick around. Not every winter was as mild as the one that had just passed. Naturally, she was right.

Perhaps this morning I'll tell my petunias it's time to grow now that the danger of frost has passed. They've been a little on the lazy side and look the same as when I planted them a month ago. I knew it was too early to stick them in the ground, but I couldn't wait. Like many other impatient gardeners, I took a chance and ended up covering the annuals most nights so they wouldn't freeze. If they don't get a move on, they'll look much the same in September as they did in May.

Ah, the bliss of summer. Brisk mornings, sunny days, picnics, campfires, cool nights, and the peaceful lap of Lake Superior as it gently touches the shore. Those of us with old bones will bask in your warmth. We'll overlook bugs that bite our arms and ignore humidity as sweat drips from our pores. Unlike tourists, we know another winter's just around the corner.

The Thrill of a Simple Sparkler

When I was a kid, we were never given fireworks more dangerous than a hand-held sparkler. As the sky darkened on the Fourth of July, Dad lit one end of the gray stick. We held the other end in our hand and had great fun twirling it in the yard. I have no recollection of running through the grass. It was usually tall. I'm sure we were warned that a spark might land on the dry grass and a devastating fire ensue. After such a dire warning, great care was taken, and we were satisfied to stand still and watch the sparkler do its thing until it fizzled out.

If we were lucky, our parents had purchased a couple boxes of those low-tech items. If not, we had to settle for whatever amount was contained in one box, maybe a dozen. If equally divided, that meant each kid got four. If one failed to sparkle, it was just too bad. My sister might have shared hers, but I was the middle child, and it's doubtful I felt obliged to hand mine over. When the sparkler fun ended, so did our Fourth. We did not attend the fireworks in Sault Ste. Marie. Mom couldn't stand the noise. Any closer than twenty miles would have deafened her, so we stayed home. Nobody pouted or whined.

We found other ways to celebrate the evening of our independence. For me that meant putting a flashlight underneath the sheet and reading a book, something I was not allowed to do. Mom said reading with such a dim light would ruin my eyes. My sister probably stayed up longer and tried to get a glimpse of the night sky as it lit up with colorful explosives from surrounding towns. My brother most likely went to his room and shot his cap gun until he ran out of the little red strip of caps.

Much has changed since the days of my youth, but one thing has remained constant. I do not seek out firework displays. Like my mother, the loud noise overrides any pleasure the brilliant works might bring. Even Miss Peggy, the cat I fell heir to four years ago, is terrified of thunder and seeks out a hiding place. I can't imagine what she'll do if she hears the blast of Cherry Bombs, M-80s, and a myriad of other explosives breaking the peace and quiet of a July evening on our normally quiet sideroad.

I understand people want to celebrate our independence by shooting off fireworks. I suppose it's long been a tradition of showing how advanced we are. We moved from a simple sparkler in our front yard to an enormous display of multi-colored designs in the night sky. It brings delight to young children and fond memories to adults.

Throughout the day, there are parades, picnics, and the anticipation of the night's entertainment. What's a little noise? It only lasts an hour and comes around once a year. Let's enjoy it while we still have something to celebrate. Whether you stay home and watch spectacular displays on your digital device or join the crowds along the riverfront, have a wonderful Fourth of July.

The Dog Days of August

August has a special feel to it unmatched by any other month. The lazy dog days melt seamlessly into one another until it's hard to tell where one ends and the other begins. At least, that's the way it was when I was young. Cumulus clouds filled the sky, hay was harvested, vegetables canned, and Mom shopped for our school clothes at Montgomery Wards.

The 15th of August is the day Catholics celebrate the Assumption of Mary into heaven. I don't know if the tradition continues, but when I was growing up we always went to mass to mark the occasion. But there's another reason why that date is memorable, and it has nothing to do with religion. It has to do with Broken Horn, Mom's favorite Hereford. I was twelve years old and remember that day as if it were yesterday.

The other cows had freshened in early spring like they're supposed to, but Broken Horn wasn't due until August. For weeks Mom had walked down the road to the field where our Herefords were pastured during summer. She regularly checked on Broken Horn to make sure everything was okay as her due date neared. When Mom didn't see her, she was convinced something was wrong, so on the 15th our relatives rallied and helped us comb the pasture and the woods behind it where the cattle often roamed. I stayed with Mom. I don't remember how long we walked and called the cow's name, but the memory of what we found has stayed with me to this day.

We were walking along the stream where clover and wild Rose of Sharon grew when we entered a quiet spot where the cows rested in the shade of the trees. It was cool and everything was still. There was a feeling of peace in that clearing, kind of like the way a church feels on Sunday mornings before it fills with people. Mom was a few steps ahead of me, holding branches aside so they wouldn't fly back and hit me in the face. Red tuffs of hair were snagged on some of the branches where cows had pushed their way through. Rust-colored pine needles carpeted the forest floor. Purple wildflowers circled the area, and maidenhair ferns were everywhere.

What I remember most about that day is the smell. Without warning, a gentle breeze stirred the air and brought an unpleasant odor. I started complaining about the stench when Mom silenced me. She strained her head to one side as if listening to something. I did likewise, but all I could hear were birds and the rustle of leaves as the breeze ran through them. Then I heard the moans. They were getting closer but not stronger like the smell. I reached for Mom's hand and her fingers locked with mine. We took a few more steps and then we were there, facing the sight we had hoped God would spare us. Mom dropped my hand and ran to the animals. I stood alone and watched as she cried "Broken Horn" in a voice that told me the house would be very quiet that night and there would be no going to mass.

Mom said to get Dad and I ran from the clearing. I remember the shrill of my whistle breaking the silence of the woods. I kept yelling for Dad, but all I heard was the echo of the whistle and my words as they bounced back to me and all I saw was the sight in the clearing. Broken Horn's calf, a big, beautiful blood-red heifer, was next to her but she wasn't breathing. She was dead, probably had been for days, and the crows had been feasting. Broken Horn lay on her side and didn't stop moaning even when Mom put her arms around the cow's neck.

If you're like me, some scenes from your childhood are permanently etched in your mind's eye and no matter how hard you try, you can't remove them. There's no "delete" button to erase the memory. Dad and my uncles buried the calf, but I didn't stay around to see it. Somehow, they managed to roll Broken Horn onto a low trailer and bring her home. Mom called the vet, but when he saw the cow he said there wasn't anything he could do, and the kindest thing would be to put her out of her misery. I was in my playhouse when I heard the shot from Dad's rifle.

Whenever the 15th rolls around, I remember that August day of long ago. The field where Broken Horn's calf died is a forest now, filled with maple and spruce trees, a few birch and a scattering of red pines. My brother's home is just down the road from me, nestled among the trees that overtook the pasture. The path once leading to the gate is now a driveway. The fences are gone, the beavers dammed the river so not even a stream remains, and the ground will never again grow hay.

Although I had seen dead cats and dogs, their passing didn't bother me as much as Broken Horn's and her calf. I cried the day we found them because I imagined Broken Horn had suffered knowing she couldn't help her baby. She had to watch it die. Dad said the calf was probably stillborn, but I didn't believe that. I figured getting born was just too much for it and it gave up before ever trying to live. I thought maybe Broken Horn had tried to coax it to life, but I guessed she was all worn out, too, and she knew it was too late to save either one of them. Such were the thoughts that passed through my mind according to an entry in my old diary.

For the rest of that month, life on the sideroad continued as before, but I never forgot that warm afternoon when I heard the sorrow in Mom's voice. I don't remember where Jude was, but I know she was too pragmatic to have bothered with tears. All these years later, I can almost hear her say, "For crying out loud, you two, it's only a dead calf and cow. Why all the fuss?" Then she would have helped with the burying, gone in the house, made a baloney sandwich, and sang along with Elvis.

Such are the memories of one dog day in August.

Another School Year Beckons

Summer slipped away like warm rain running down a drainpipe. Gentle autumn breezes carried wildflower seeds in all directions, ensuring next year's pastures would be abundant with Queen Anne's lace, sweet clover, daisies, and wild yellow mustard. School bells clanged the opening of another academic year. Girls were dressed in new corduroy jumpers, white blouses, and saddle oxfords. Boys stood like soldiers in stiff new denim jeans and sturdy lace-up shoes. Like condemned prisoners, we waited at the end of our lanes for the buses to pick us up and carry us away to the dreaded schoolhouse.

Gone were carefree mornings when we burrowed deep into our feather pillows, ignoring alarm clocks awaking our parents. When we finally got up and finished our daily chores, the river beckoned. Fishing rods appeared, swimming trunks were patched and ready, and modest swimsuits were carefully chosen by concerned mothers. Those of us who didn't swim spent all afternoon picking berries in the fields or riding our bicycles down the road, leaving a trail of dust behind us.

July strawberries had been picked and spun into jam. The blueberries, blackberries, and raspberries of August all met the same doom in cauldrons of boiling fruit syrup and sugar. For days the fire blazed in the woodstove, turning our kitchen into a sauna as jar after jar of fruits and vegetables were canned and neatly placed on our pantry shelves. Each new quart and pint announced the passing of summer. Some of us were eager for the new school year. Some were ambivalent, and some were downright terrified.

As I waited for the bus with my sister and brother, lots of thoughts swirled in my mind. Would I have to sit alone on the ride to school or would somebody sit with me? What if I didn't like my teachers or nobody liked me? Would the kids laugh because I had shot up another three inches and my fingers had grown at least one inch? Was my jumper okay or should I have worn a dress? Did my new shoes make my feet look longer? Would anyone notice the scar on my right arm that stuck out like a black licorice stain on a pink skirt?

My heart often beat a little faster when I heard the roar of the bus. As I watched it turn the corner and head towards us, the driver barreled down the road, and woe to the cat or dog that crossed his path. When he screeched to a halt at our stop, we knew what was coming.

Over the years, we had a number of bus drivers who were polite and waited until we found a seat before stepping on the gas, but not Mean Mac. He was a young fellow who delighted in pressing hard on the gas pedal as soon as he closed the door behind us. Unsuspecting newcomers got a surprise when the bus jumped forward and sent them flying down the aisle to the amusement of the driver and the kids already safely in their seats. It was a five-mile drive from our place to the schoolhouse in Brimley, but sometimes it seemed like fifty, especially when no one sat next to me. In the time it took to pick up all the kids, I traveled miles through the solitary labyrinth of my mind. If I sat alone, I always looked out the window. I imagined all sorts of things, especially what it would be like to experience an endless summer. If another kid sat beside me, my daydreaming continued, and I remained oblivious to the chatter of my seatmate.

When we finally arrived at school and entered our classroom, everything looked new and shiny. The floors were slippery from many coats of wax. The desks and blackboard were scrubbed clean. The alphabet above the blackboard was neatly tacked to the wall. If we weren't commanded to sit in alphabetical order, I always gravitated to a desk by the window. There I could sneak a peek at where I wanted to be—outside in the fresh air instead of in a stuffy classroom.

The week following Labor Day was a week of transition. Some of us handled it better than others, especially if each day brought rain. It was easier to put away the distractions of summer when autumn rain and wind announced harsh weather was not far behind. When I saw fallow fields or red leaves on maple trees, I knew it was time to say goodbye to our three-month vacation and turn my attention to history, geography, and the worst subject of all, arithmetic.

My school days are long behind me, but memories still linger. The years I spent studying at universities are mostly forgotten. It's the years between kindergarten and twelfth grade that are the most clear. The many hours spent in those classrooms are partly responsible for my personality. My peers, the teachers, the books, and the social activities associated with school played an important role in molding me into the adult I have become. But sometimes I wonder how any of us make it through the long years of our formal schooling. There are so many things to worry about other than class assignments. School has changed a lot since I was a kid, but I don't think kids have changed all that much. Most still suffer from feelings of inferiority, much as I did as a youngster. A pretty girl or handsome boy can be just as insecure as the class clown who pretends he doesn't have a care in the world or give a hoot about the opinion of others.

Anyone willing to put in the required time and money can graduate from college, but it takes more than a degree to be content with the hand life deals us. It takes knowing we are worthwhile regardless of the size of our house or paycheck. If every evening we go to sleep knowing we've done the best we can and harmed no one along the way, we are more successful than King Midas and all his gold. If that lesson is taught in today's public schools, we don't have to worry about the future of our country. It's going to be just fine.

Any Halloween Candy Left?

If there's one thing that bothers me about Halloween, it's all those candy bars I have to consume because no little kids stop by my place. Perhaps if I turned on an outside light, witches, goblins, or clowns might stop, but my light hasn't worked in years. I suppose I could decorate with pumpkins and fairy lights and hang a "Welcome" sign on my front door, but that's a lot of work. So I guess there's nothing to do but the inevitable, and you know what that is.

Every Halloween some of us have the same dilemma. We know perfectly well no one is going to knock on our door, but just to be on the safe side we buy bags of candy. And it's always the good stuff. No Jolly Ranchers or Tootsie Rolls for us. It's only the best for any would-be Trick or Treaters. Naturally, we purchase what we like in case we're stuck with it. If you're like me, you tend to buy the candy as soon as it begins appearing in the stores. It's only natural we want to be prepared. Buy early and we won't have any regrets when the 31st rolls around and the shelves are empty.

Only problem with that idea is we have to sample the candy to make sure it's fit for human consumption. One Almond Joy leads to another. One Hershey's Kiss leads to a couple more. And nobody can eat just one little KitKat without eating four. We don't want stale treats, so we have no choice but to unwrap some Snickers and enjoy them with a cup of coffee. By the time the middle of October is upon us, we make another trip to the store and buy more candy. We leave it in the car so we're not tempted to eat it, but then we worry that mice might be hiding underneath the seats, just waiting for the chance to nibble open a bag and destroy the contents. So, of course, we bring the candy into the house and hide it in the unused roaster in the pantry.

What's that you say? No roaster? No pantry? Well then, hide the bags in a closet. No, not your bedroom closet or the broom closet or the one that smells like mothballs. Okay, closets are not a good idea. Hide the bags in something you never use. No, for goodness sake not in the Hoover. You might take a notion to vacuum. Imagine the mess you'll find yourself in as you separate dust bunnies and dog hair from candy bars. The more we search for hiding places, the more we realize there's only one logical solution. We must not buy anything until the 30th. That way we're sure to have candy for any little beggars who knock on our door.

Years ago, there were only a few stores that sold Halloween candy, and the supply was limited. However, now that Walmart and Meijer are here we have candy galore. There's never a shortage, but if we purchase too many bags, there's no need to fret. We know all that candy will be long gone before Thanksgiving. Our insatiable love of sweets will ensure nothing goes to waste.

Lunch, Anyone?

Recently a friend invited me to lunch. Tina and I have been friends since kindergarten. Once a month we meet at a restaurant, catch up on what's happening in our lives and reminisce about our school days. We're both single, which means we don't answer to anyone. We relax and visit over coffee and dessert for two hours and nobody tell us to get a move on. But this time when Tina called, her invitation was more like a request. For a year, an old acquaintance had been trying to pluck up the courage to renew their friendship. He finally called her and mentioned he would like to meet for lunch on Friday.

Tina wanted me to accompany her in case things got a little testy. I'm pretty good at handling potentially awkward situations if they don't last too long.

We dolled up and met at the restaurant in the local casino. It was a little past noon, and I wondered where her friend was. Sometimes a fellow loses track of time if he finds a lucky slot machine, so we decided to get a booth and wait. Imagine our surprise when we saw her friend with his friend already seated and working on their desserts. What a peculiar date, I thought. Tina was a little hesitant to say anything, but I wasn't. I asked the boys if they wanted us to join them or would they rather we sat at the table across from their booth. Looks of amazement on their faces matched ours, but they graciously invited us to sit with them. We made our salad selections from the buffet and returned to the booth. To say the least, conversation was forced, but we mumbled along as best as we could.

These boys graduated high school four years ahead of us. They didn't recognize me, and I had no idea who they were. One bore a slight resemblance to Clint Eastwood and the other to Telly Savalas. After Tina introduced me, my memory was jogged and I remembered Clint. Although a little altered, he was still the good-looking boy who rode our school bus and always sat in the third seat behind the driver. I recalled Clint's perfect posture and his inability to smile. I think I was slightly afraid of him, but when I was young, I was afraid of everybody so that was no big deal.

Telly was harder to recall because he rode a different bus. I vaguely remembered him as a tall, blond fellow. He was still tall, but his hair had fled along with his youth. We seated ourselves—Tina next to Telly and I next to Clint. Telly was talkative and Clint managed a grin. As folks do when they don't know what to say, we inquired about the years since leaving school. We agreed they were just fine. Of course we were lying. Altogether, our divorces numbered seven, our children numbered nine, and our combined finances didn't amount to a pinch of salt. This information was gleaned through creative questioning on my part. Probably due to his shyness, Clint had remained a bachelor with no children. His contribution to the conversation was limited to positive remarks on the meal and observations on which slot machine was giving a good return. Our coffee arrived about the same time as their bill. Telly volunteered to pay for our lunch, but Tina said no, we would handle it.

We all shook hands and said it was wonderful seeing everybody again. Continuing to lie, we said the years had been kind to us, that we hadn't changed much, that we still had our good looks and personalities, and that it was a real pleasure getting together. Although no future plans were discussed, we knew we would meet again soon, maybe even enjoy the restaurant's Thanksgiving buffet.

As soon as the boys were out of earshot, Tina and I couldn't contain our laughter. We giggled like schoolgirls. "What kind of date was that?" I finally managed to ask. Who invites you to lunch then eats without you? When we recovered from another fit of laughter, I asked more questions. Tina finally admitted Telly had called three weeks earlier and mentioned they should meet "one day" for lunch. No definite date had been set. Apparently, Telly's casual invitation was just a passing whim, but it gave us a good laugh and a brilliant idea for meeting new people.

The next time we entered a restaurant, we decided to survey the room and mosey over to the most pleasant looking fellows. We would pretend that we knew them and join them for lunch. Many folks our age have hazy memories and would be too polite to tell us to get lost. It would be an ideal way to turn strangers into friends even if only for the duration of a meal. Naturally, we'd pay our own bill, but the cost would be insignificant compared to the fun we'd have. So, if one day you're dining in the Brimley area and notice two old gals approaching your booth, move over. We're about to join you for lunch and laughter.

Describing the Perfect Thanksgiving

Thanksgiving is one of those wonderful holidays when families and friends gather together and share a delicious meal. It's a great time to reconnect with loved ones, reminisce about events of the past year, and introduce new babies to all the relatives. Every television, newspaper, and magazine advertisement shows the same thing—well-dressed people clapping as the hostess deposits the twenty-pound turkey in the middle of a table laden with traditional Thanksgiving Day food.

Bowls of steaming vegetables, creamy mashed potatoes piled sky high, golden gravy swimming in porcelain boats, butter melting into warm dinner rolls, a dozen different casseroles, and a sideboard buckling under the weight of desserts beckon the company to dig in and enjoy. Someone says a blessing before the feast begins. Conversation is fast and easy, and an aura of love and good humor is palpable.

At least that's the picture Norman Rockwell would have us believe, and it's one most families try to imitate with varying success, but Thanksgiving often goes like this: The turkey is drier than burnt toast, the mashed potatoes are lumpy, and the gravy is watery. In the midst of the commotion, the dinner rolls were forgotten and burned to a crisp, setting off the smoke alarm. Everybody bypassed the green bean casserole. Nobody liked the oyster stuffing. The jiggly cranberry sauce landed on the floor, and the dogs ate it.

Before dinner was served, guests stuffed themselves with peanuts, Chex mix, and colorful dinner mints. Some relatives arrived fully inebriated while others waited until the car was parked before they broke the seal on a bottle of Seagram's 7. Some fought over which football game to watch. Others wanted to eat early so they could hunt before dark. Some cousins got along great. Others got out the boxing gloves. Babies cried. Dogs barked. Feathers flew.

Old uncles refused to smoke on the porch and ignored the ashtrays. They ground out their cigars in fancy candy dishes. Old aunts, rouged to look like Kewpie dolls and doused in buckets of Tabu, hugged terrified toddlers. Everybody talked and nobody listened. Diverse political opinions turned into screaming matches. Country kin, dressed in plaid flannel shirts and bib overalls, repulsed their highfalutin' city relatives dressed to the nines. Children seated at the kids' table started a food fight. When the day finally ended and the front door slammed behind the last guest, the hostess collapsed in a chair and said "never again."

The moral of this story is be happy if you're alone on Thanksgiving Day. Give thanks you're not surrounded by a bunch of snobby relatives or false friends. Don't believe the hype surrounding the holidays and get upset because you're on your own. Embrace your solitude, order Chinese take-out, and watch your favorite television shows.

Chin up. Next Thanksgiving you might find yourself in the middle of a mob and wish you had stayed home.

Choosing Christmas Wrapping Paper

Christmas wrapping paper is a booming business for the companies that make the colorful rolls. It's not like the old days when there wasn't much variety. Santa Claus, his elves, or a winter scene with reindeer and evergreens was about the limit. Now there's an endless supply of paper with every holiday theme imaginable. For a classier, more elegant look, some folks ditch Santa and Rudolph for the sleek sheen of paper bearing a strong resemblance to tin foil.

At one time I, too, joined the crowd who drank the Kool-Aid demanding we must have exceptional wrapping paper for special occasions. I thought it was quite vogue to use the most expensive and luxurious paper I could find. Same goes for bows and other decorations on the beautifully wrapped presents. Then one year I awoke from my Kool-Aid induced stupor and realized I was often spending more money on the wrapping than on the gift.

When common sense finally kicks in, we're usually amazed at how easily we're fooled and how gullible we are. Even when wrapping paper is not the main focus of a television or magazine advertisement, we can't help but notice what's underneath the Christmas tree. Have you ever seen a haphazardly wrapped gift void of ribbons and bows? Have you ever seen one that didn't glitter as the tree lights hit it? No, of course not. Our eyes spy the boxes surrounding the magnificently decorated tree, and we're intrigued at what they contain. Realistically, we know they're empty. They're nothing more than props, but they're effective in convincing us our gifts should look just as spectacular. Nobody wants to give a present wrapped in cheap paper. I suppose kids don't care, but adults do. I know that's a sweeping statement and it's not true in all cases, but think about it. Even if wrapping paper is nixed in favor of a holiday bag, it must be of the highest caliber. The handles and bottoms of cheap bags come unglued if the gift weighs more than an ounce. I found that out the hard way.

What's a person to do to solve the gift wrap dilemma? Well, as usual, I don't know, but I'll make a stab at it and offer some suggestions. I was thirty when I received a birthday present wrapped in a page torn from the Detroit telephone book. The fellow in my life at the time was a starving artist. He could barely afford a present let alone a roll of exotic wrapping paper for a gift the size of a walnut. Did it bother me that a 14k gold pinky ring engraved with our initials in Greek was stuck in a tiny box wrapped in the Yellow Pages? No. I wore that ring long after I had traded George in for another artist. The new guy was a lot thinner and called himself a poet. My gift that year was wrapped in a Shakespeare sonnet that had been ripped from a book most likely borrowed from and never returned to a library.

Over the years, my presents were wrapped in lunch bags, old socks, White Castle napkins, shoebox tissue paper, and empty Kool-Aid envelopes. When I gave a present tucked inside a clean cat food can and wrapped in Charmin, my friends cheered. I had finally joined the Wrapping Paper Rebels. Membership is free and open to everyone.

Nuts Are for Fruitcakes

"Christmas is coming, the goose is getting fat. Please put a penny in the old man's hat." That silly rhyme is no stranger to those of us who learned it as a child. The poem continued by saying if a penny wasn't available then a ha'penny was suggested as an alternative. If that meager amount was too much, the poem ended by asking a blessing on the poor beggar who had even less than the old man. For readers who might wonder if this is an introduction leading to an appeal for alms, the answer is no. Although Christmas is coming, I haven't the slightest intention of purchasing a goose, a turkey, a ham, or any other creature that walked on two or four legs. My holiday dinner will be vegetarian. Dessert will be a fruitcake, the only cake that gets shoved to the back of the fridge and remains there for at least a year. When eventually discovered, it shows no sign of spoilage because even mold won't touch it. Why fruitcake is the poor relation to every other cake and gets a bum rap every year is beyond me. When prepared properly, it's absolutely delicious.

I agree that red and green maraschino cherries riddled with preservatives are unappetizing. So are glazed orange and lemon peels. Such a mess does belong in the back of the refrigerator to be consumed only out of desperation. When there's not another sweet in the house and we crave sugar, then and only then will the fruitcake emerge. A thoughtful spouse will camouflage it with a smear of white icing or soak it overnight in a rum bath.

But those of us who have fiddled around with the recipe until it makes sense to our taste buds know how to turn a culinary disaster into a triumph. A long time ago I realized all I had to do was add the ingredients I liked instead of the traditional ones the recipe call for. Prior to baking the cake, I chop and combine dates, pecans, walnuts, hazelnuts, and almonds. I add some plump raisins and douse everything with orange juice and brandy. Every few hours, I give the mixture a good stir and let it sit overnight on the kitchen counter. When the fruit and nuts have absorbed all the liquid, I make the batter, adding molasses and lots of spices. I've used the same recipe since 1983. I don't use as many raisins as it calls for because I don't like them, and I certainly don't add the mixed candied fruit. I double the amount of spices, add more nuts, and sometimes use whole wheat flour. I never use margarine, and I always add brown sugar. Other than these few modifications, the recipe is identical to the one in the cookbook.

My high school home economics teacher, Mrs. McIver, tried her best to teach us girls how to "put up" fruit and vegetables, turn grape juice into jelly, create a fabulous Chinese Pot Roast, and make a Victory Fruitcake. Her reasoning was simple. She was preparing us to be homemakers. I learned how to can and jam and sew and bake and continued to practice these skills long after graduation. During the holiday season, I used her recipes for Christmas Sugar Cookies and Divine Divinity Fudge. I often baked Light as Air Baking Powder Biscuits to go with the Chinese Pot Roast, but there was one recipe I never attempted and that was Stuffed Lobster Tails. For reasons known only to Mrs. Mac, she bought the frozen tails and showed us how to prepare them. I have no idea where she found them and even less idea why she thought country girls would be interested in something from the ocean when we were surrounded by freshwater yielding whitefish, perch, and trout.

During my senior year, I won the Betty Crocker Homemaker of Tomorrow award. In other words, I knew the proper way to dust furniture, set a table, make a white sauce, and bake a dessert. Teenage girls of today would expire laughing at the things our teacher thought were important, but they don't know what they're missing. After all these years, I still have fond memories of just about everything Mrs. Mac taught us except her Victory Fruitcake. As with her lobster tail recipe, the fruitcake one also went by the wayside. According to a stained index card I found in my old recipe box, I was in the ninth grade when we attempted this holiday staple.

I coaxed Mom into making it a few days before Christmas. We got out our largest cast iron frying pan and lined it with a brown paper bag cut to size. I rubbed lard into the pan and the paper. In those days, there was no such thing as parchment paper, at least not in the stores of Sault Ste. Marie. Mom's Sunbeam probably couldn't handle the batter's weight so most likely Dad was called away from his barn chores and asked to stir the brown cement, wrestle it into the pan, and put it in the oven.

Through many years of experience, Mom knew her way around a woodstove. Although there was no dial on the oven door indicating the temperature inside, she made sure the heat remained constant. Once the cake was in the oven, it was left alone for at least two hours. When a fruitcake was baking, we were allowed to walk at a normal pace in the kitchen, even jump or stomp or chase the cat if the urge came over us kids. Regular cakes had a tendency to fall from the slightest kitchen commotion so we tiptoed around, but a fruitcake was hardy. Nothing bothered it because it didn't rise any higher than a whisper. When a delicious, inviting aroma filled our kitchen, Mom decided the cake had baked long enough and carefully removed it from the oven. Long before they became fashionable, Dad made birch wood trivets. The fiery hot pan was placed upon one and left to cool. Eventually, the cake was removed and the paper peeled away.

I wish I could say we had baked a masterpiece. I wish I had fond memories of a gloriously moist cake gracing our Christmas table that year, but I don't. What I remember is a blackened, rock hard piece of artillery no human could consume without mortal consequences. We tried to fix it with a slather of frosting and red cinnamon dots, but it was hopeless. Gram usually baked our fruitcakes. Hers were regarded with respect and admiration and even requested as wedding cakes, but I had insisted we bake Mrs. Mac's recipe because it was a winner.

Don't ask me what became of that holiday treat. It might have been fed to the pigs or maybe Dad used it to level a leaning shed. What I do recall is Mom saying Victory Fruitcake hadn't quite lived up to its name. It was many years before I tried making another fruitcake, and believe me, I didn't try that old recipe. I was living in Detroit and wanted to impress my city friends so I prepared a date and nut cake full of spices and Brer Rabbit molasses. Then I made a brandy sauce, poured it over the cake, and put a lit match to it. The effect was stunning. Mrs. Mac would have been proud. This country girl had come a long way from the sideroad and her teacher's World War II fruitcake recipe.

Part III:
Sharing
Common Experiences

Monitored by a Little Green Dot

For years I had a Facebook account but didn't do much with it. I glanced at it every few months, but I wasn't really interested in what people ate for lunch or how many puppies their dog had. I didn't join any groups, share any posts, or believe news stories coming from Onion. I don't remember when I decided to hop on the fast-moving media train, but hop I did and now I'm hooked.

Once a hook is in you, it's difficult to remove. Just ask any fish unfortunate enough to swallow a hook and swim away. I imagine it will suffer a painful death, but I don't know for sure. Maybe a fisherman will enlighten me. Anyway, I now merrily check my FaceBook (FB) newsfeed every morning while drinking my coffee and enjoying a muffin. Merrily, that is, until I learned there's a little green dot telling people I'm awake and open for business.

Egad, I thought. My time on FB is being monitored. Folks know when I click on and how long I stay on when I forget to click out. My friends probably think I have nothing better to do than remain on the site all day. This is nuts. It's worse than an ankle bracelet. When a person is monitored by the legal system, he has more privacy than a FB user. Who decided to tell everyone when we arise and when we go to bed?

I've said for a long time the age we live in is wacky. We're in a losing battle with technology. Unlike wars fought on battlegrounds, one side has a chance of beating the physical enemy, but how are we supposed to win a digital battle?

I don't want that green dot telling everyone I finally rolled out of bed at 8:00 a.m. My FBF might think I'm lazy. I don't want the dot telling them I retired at midnight and got up at 3:00 a.m. because I couldn't sleep. What if someone sees the dot and wants to come over for an early morning visit? The chances of that happening are slim because I don't encourage visitors, but we never know. Some lonely soul might think it's a good idea to slip on a housecoat and slippers and pull into my driveway.

I've always liked the color green. It's fresh and clean and comes in a variety of shades. It reminds me of a perfectly mowed lawn or the stems of beautiful flowers, the leaves on trees, and even the changing hues of the Great Lakes. Green denotes nature at its finest. But Facebook's green dot doesn't remind me of anything remotely related to nature. It's a digital spy, a hook that has got to go. Someone please tell me how to remove it before I cancel my account and slip back to the old days when something as invasive as FB was, for me, as remote as Mars.

Ready, Set, Turn: Daylight Saving Time

We humans are an odd lot. Twice a year we interrupt the natural rhythm of our body by turning our clocks forward or backward. It doesn't make sense and never has. Why we fiddle with time is another one of life's many mysteries I'll never understand. I know we're supposed to embrace daylight at 10 p.m. That's fine if we're retired, but what about the people who have to roll out of bed an hour earlier than usual?

Years ago I suppose I was glad daylight was still with me when I cut the grass at 9:30 p.m. Older golfers are probably delighted they can swing their clubs well past their usual bedtime. Most kids don't play outdoors during the day let alone well into the evening, so a few more hours of daylight during summer means nothing to them. When workers get up before the sun does, they might be more interested in relaxing in their favorite chair when they get home than in going to the beach.

Obviously, my resistance to change is showing again. I can't help it. I like things to stay as they are. That's why I still have battery-operated clocks hanging on my walls. Sure, they take double A batteries that need to be replaced every six months, but that's a minor inconvenience. I don't have to constantly charge a smart phone that isn't smart enough to recharge itself, at least I don't think such phones exist but I could be mistaken. The digital world moves at breakneck speed while I move at a snail's pace. I keep old wristwatches because they're efficient if I remember to wind them, and they don't require a third hand like a cell phone does.

I appreciate many modern conveniences, but messing with time is not one of them. Time isn't a convenience. It's something we spend from the cradle to the grave. Some of us accomplish nothing as we while away the hours and wait for the day to end. Other folks are constantly alert to the passing minutes. They accomplish great things, but the majority of us plod along day-to-day as we wait for the weekend and freedom from our place of employment.

For many people, retirement comes as a shock. They're used to enduring the same monotonous routine and after a few weeks of being idle, they don't know what to do with their time. If they can't find suitable employment, the last thing they want is another hour of daylight to remind them of the months and years ahead of them with nothing on their hands but time.

My unsolicited suggestion is relax, retirees. Find a comfortable chair and watch the day slowly fade away. And for folks just starting out in the workforce, your body will eventually adjust to the time change. You might even enjoy that extra hour of daylight before nodding off to dreamland. And remember, in eight months DST will end and the time-controlling gods will once again rule unfettered and unchallenged as your body struggles to readjust to another time change.

When All Else Fails, Try Avon or Cake Decorating

Throughout the years, most of the women I've had the pleasure of meeting had two things in common. At one time or another they all tried their hand at selling Avon products and when that idea fizzled, they took a cake decorating class. I have to admit I'm part of the sisterhood that did both.

In the 1980s I decided to become an Avon lady. I'm not sure what possessed me to think I would be good at sales, but I suppose it was a matter of necessity. Although I was a crackerjack legal secretary and had worked at some of the most prestigious law firms in Detroit as well as working as a speechwriter for former U.S. Senator Donald Riegle, when I moved to Sault Ste. Marie I couldn't get a job interview let alone an offer of employment. So I paid the $20 fee requested by an Avon recruiter and thought I was on my way to building an empire. My empire consisted of boxes of cosmetics and colognes stacked in a corner of the basement of my apartment. I think the enterprise collapsed when I tried to hawk a cologne called "Breathless." It's a story worth sharing.

My nephew, Alan, was seven years old at the time and suffered from childhood asthma. He was home-schooled. One day I decided to take him with me when I made my rounds. It was the equivalent of the popular "Accompany an Adult to Work Day" often promoted in public schools. I thought it would be an excellent learning experience for Alan to see a saleswoman at work.

Unlike some gals who sold to the people in their office, I went door-to-door just like sales reps of the 1950s. It never occurred to me that very few women would be home during the day because most held a full-time job outside the house. I was thinking of the old days when Mom looked forward to the arrival of her Avon lady. While Mom pored over the brochure, Daisy drank tea and told Mom all the latest gossip. It was a social call initiated by sales, and Mom enjoyed every minute of it. My sister and I loved the lipsticks and other samples the representative left.

But I began my Avon career thirty years later, and it didn't take long to realize I was facing an uphill battle. However, on the day I took my nephew with me, I was confident we would find at least one person who would welcome us into her kitchen. As Alan and I tramped down Augusta Street, he kept asking when this magical person would appear. We had walked up one street and down another and he was getting tired. I probably told him to have faith. Eventually our rap would be answered and the sales pitch could begin.

Finally, we knocked on the right door. A lovely stay-at-home mother smiled and invited us in. We walked into her living room like victorious soldiers marching into a conquered city. As the young woman brought refreshments, I placed jars of face creams and bottles of nail polish on her coffee table. I lined up an assortment of hand lotions, shampoos, and bubble bath. I opened a uniquely designed plastic container filled with tiny plastic tubes of lipstick samples. Finally, I brought out the piece de résistance—fancy bottles containing Avon's famous colognes.

Our hostess examined everything while Alan ate cookies and amused her child, and I explained the merits of my products. Everything was going well until I sprayed the latest cologne, a $15 bottle of Breathless. I pointed the nozzle high in the air and showered the room with a fragrance that can only be described as a first cousin to Raid. When the scent of fly dope filled the small room, Alan's asthma flared up. He was gasping for breath as I was praising the merits of Breathless.

Need I say more? We beat a hasty retreat. I have no idea if I made a sale that day, but I do remember Alan saying the cologne sure lived up to its name. Shortly after that unfortunate episode, I resigned my position and didn't return to Avon sales for another ten years. By that time, Breathless was long gone, Alan was seventeen and over his asthma, and never again did I invite a youngster to accompany me.

My cake decorating days didn't fare much better. It was 1997 and I was itching to begin a new career. I figured once I mastered the art of decorating birthday cakes for friends and family, I could jump to wedding cakes. Then I could quit my job as a substitute teacher and make a living decorating cakes. I signed up for a class at Joanne Fabrics. I purchased all the necessary supplies and arrived early on the appointed evening. There were six other girls in the class. We brought our cakes and were eager to begin, but first we had to get the cakes out of the pans. This presented a challenge for gals who had neglected to coat their fancy cake pans with half an inch of lard. Our instructor was encouraging. So what if the cake didn't want to release from the Mickey Mouse pan? So what if it came out in sixteen pieces? No matter. Great gobs of frosting would hold it together.

Like fearless warriors, we charged into the decorating fray, except for one girl whose cake refused to exit the pan. With tears of embarrassment running down her cheeks, she grabbed her stuff and went home. The rest of us anxiously awaited the next step, which involved preparing the icing. I wondered why we had been instructed to bring a small container of Crisco Shortening. What did that have to do with anything, I asked myself. It didn't take long to discover the answer. The lady teaching the class told us to combine the Crisco with the confectioner's sugar we had brought. It never occurred to me that shortening was essential in icing. That it was mandatory if we wanted our cakes to look like the ones purchased from a display case in a supermarket. Although the thought of mixing shortening and sugar was disgusting, when food coloring was added it was easier to overlook the fact that we were decorating our cakes with hydrogenated vegetable oil.

Once the colored sugar and Crisco were spooned into a pastry tube, I was in for another surprise. I had no idea it would take the strength of a sumo wrestler to squeeze them out. Our instructor also neglected to caution us that extreme repetitive squeezing might lead to carpal tunnel. You guessed it. My cake decorating days lasted about as long as the class—six weeks—but I kept all the paraphernalia associated with the business. I had purchased at least $100 worth of books, cake pans, decorative tips, and dozens of other instruments required to make cakes look beautiful. I stored everything in a kitchen drawer, but finally sold the lot for a song when I realized I would never again attempt to decorate a cake using silver tips inserted into a pastry tube filled with the equivalent of a pound of good old lard. I returned to substitute teaching, eventually earned my MA from Northern Michigan University and went on to teach English Composition at the college level.

Occasionally, I still purchase Avon products from a local rep, but the only cake decorating I do is a quick slap of chocolate frosting on a one layer, six-inch round cake destined only for me. In a lifetime of false starts, it's about all I can manage. I'm sure you're wondering if I use Crisco in the icing. Not a chance. My choice of fat was, is, and always will be butter. And it's Kerrygold, the real stuff that comes straight from some of Ireland's finest cows.

Navigating the Minefield of Words

Do you ever feel like every time you open your mouth you say the wrong thing? I don't know why it is, but some folks have a knack for offending people without intending to. We don't think before we speak. We just say what's on our mind without any regard to how our words will sound in the ears of the listener. Other people have a gift for pleasing everyone even if they're actually insulting them. Call it charm or manipulation, we all know folks who can get away with the most outlandish remarks. If we said the same things, they would be considered mean, offensive, or downright rude.

Dad had the natural wit of an true Irishman. He could disarm anyone as fast as Ali could deliver a one-two punch. Dad insulted relatives with such grace and humor they didn't realize they were being made sport of until they got home and thought about it. Then it was too late to retaliate. I wish I could say I inherited Dad's easy, cheerful blarney, but such is not always the case.

I'll give you a few examples. When I was about ten, the phone company ran a party line down my sideroad. Our number was 38J, either two shorts and one long or one long and two shorts. I don't remember. Anyway, using the phone was a privilege, not the mandatory third appendage it is today. In other words, I didn't grow up with a telephone and to this day do not enjoy talking on one. About a month ago I mentioned my indifference regarding the phone to an acquaintance and haven't heard from her since. Then there's the bossy lady friend who got on my nerves. She often called me unpleasant names, but I overlooked her insults for a long time because when she wasn't being obnoxious, she was funny. Then one day she stretched my tolerance to the max, and I returned a dose of her own medicine. That was five years ago. No word from her since then, either.

Turning the clock way back to 1986, a relative thought I should get out more and invited me to her weekly Al Anon meeting. Against my better judgment, I agreed and attended a few sessions. I kept quiet as I listened to the women gripe about their husbands. Week after week it was the same thing. The men left the toilet seat up. They tracked in mud from their construction jobs. They didn't spend enough time with the kids. They didn't hang on every word their wife said. They wouldn't help with household chores. They had to be dragged to church every Sunday. They were tired from their rotating shift work. They weren't romantic enough. They snored. Finally, I couldn't stand it any longer and told the gals if I was married to one of them, I'd drink too. You can just about imagine how that went over.

Sometimes I think the only solution to keeping everyone happy is to keep quiet, but even silence is capable of angering people. When I was a freshman at what is now Lake Superior State University in Sault Ste. Marie, I was a timid country mouse. I probably thought the best way to go unnoticed in class was to say nothing. I never joined in the discussions and never asked questions. I was so shy I thought I could become invisible if I kept my mouth shut. That idea failed miserably.

I remember a social studies class held in Brown Hall. Instead of desks, we sat around a table much like King Arthur and his Knights. Semesters eventually replaced terms, but in 1966 terms comprised an academic year. By the end of the term, I had not spoken one word in class. Although verbal participation was a required element for determining our grade, I was too apprehensive to open my mouth even when I thought I might have something of value to say. Timid students know the longer they wait to express their thoughts, the more scared they become because they know all eyes will be on them. What I didn't know then was it's better to say something stupid during the first few days of class and get it over with. Then if we occasionally contribute a different, but viable viewpoint, we're seen as deep thinkers instead of mute dunces.

Unknown to me, my reserve in that class irritated a fellow female student from Canada. During the last week of class, she voiced her frustration at my hesitancy to speak. She turned to me and asked why I had not offered an opinion during the entire term. I felt my face flame red and wanted to disappear, to simply evaporate. Obviously, there was no way I was going to spontaneously vanish. I endured her annoyance like a sheep going to slaughter. She was angry and disgusted with me, which drove me further into my shell. That incident occurred fifty-seven years ago. It's the only comment I remember from any of my college classes. That's the enduring power of words.

Expressing an opinion can be compared to walking through a linguistic minefield. If we say too much, we've hurt someone's feelings. If we say nothing, we've let others hurt ours, or have silently agreed with an opposing viewpoint. What's a person to do? I don't know, but I keep hoping one of these days Dad's droll genes will visit me before I die. Mom always said he could charm the rattle out of a snake while all she could get from it was a bite.

Until I find a happy medium, I suppose I should keep a roll of duct tape handy for self-protection. I might look silly with my mouth taped shut, but it might eliminate a lot of unnecessary problems.

No More to Play the Wild Rover

Recently, a friend stopped by to tell me he was feeling low because he had just buried his dog. As Jim spoke, his voice caught as if he couldn't get his breath, and I realized he was choking back tears. Spike was his best friend. He was always at Jim's side or riding next to him in the front seat of his truck. They were buddies. They understood each other and got along better than most people. Jim said there was only one habit Spike wouldn't give up and that was his love of greeting people, whether they were on foot, riding a bicycle, or driving a car.

Jim had been planting his garden when he heard a commotion. Before he could stop him, Spike had run down the road into the path of an oncoming vehicle. The driver had no chance to swerve and avoid hitting Spike. He helped Jim pick up the dog's broken body. Jim immediately drove him to the vet, knowing all the while it was too late, knowing that Spike was dying, but hoping against hope it wasn't so and reassuring his best friend that everything would be okay.

As Jim told me the details, tears came to my eyes. I remembered all the times Spike had run alongside me as I bicycled down the road. I remembered the summer when I walked a mile down a tangled path behind Jim's house and Spike ran ahead and then back again, making sure I was still with him. I remembered the rainy night I heard a noise on my back porch and opened the door to see a big black dog begging to come in because he was afraid of thunder and Jim wasn't home.

As memories raced through my mind, I thought how my friend must feel because his memories far outnumbered mine. He was the one who had to deal with the empty cage and the unopened bag of dog food, the toys and all the sticks littering the yard from playing fetch. He was the one who had to put away the water and food dishes, the blankets, and the doggy treats. My heart went out to him as I remembered the summer he'd lost Spike's mother to cancer. I remembered telling him that Sugar had beaten the disease by dying. She was finally free of pain, and her spirit was probably watching as

Spike was laid to rest next to her in the grassy field they both loved. As these thoughts went through my mind, I wondered why we love our pets so much our heart breaks when they die.

Jim said he wouldn't be getting another animal. I feel the same way. We're sure a pet would outlive us. We've buried many throughout the years starting when we were children on neighboring farms and awakened on summer mornings to find a cat or dog lying in a ditch, hit by a car during the night. When you live on a farm, death is a given. Dogs chase cars, cats chase rabbits, weasels wiggle their way underneath the door and into the chicken coop. Cows choke on something they find in the field. Horses get colic. Pigs suffocate their young. Chickens get their heads chopped off. It's all part of farm life, but that doesn't make it easy.

Even as I write this, I can't believe Spike is gone. His death doesn't seem real. It's the same feeling when a loved one passes. It's hard to believe we'll never see them again. I know what priests and preachers say, that the Bible assures us we'll meet on the other side. That good news should strengthen us during times of sorrow. It's a nice thought, but it's too abstract to grasp when we're hurting. It's a band-aid over a terminal disease. We're raw with pain and someone is telling us to perk up, we'll meet again, so we put on a brave face until we're alone. Then as we touch something that belonged to the one we lost, we give way to the emotions we were forced to hide from well-meaning people who filled our ears with platitudes.

It's understandable why we weep over the death of a person, but why do we feel such sorrow when a pet dies? Is it because they unconditionally accept us, never pass judgment, and always listen to our problems? My last pet was Little T. He was a good old cat. My daughter rescued him when she saw the harsh way he was being treated. The year was 1997. Mom christened him "Little T" because he was just a kitten, had never been indoors, and got into all kinds of trouble. It was winter and too cold for him to stay in the garage. As he jumped from one chair to the next, Mom said he was nothing but a nuisance, but every night he snuggled next to her and during the day his favorite place to sleep was on her lap.

It will take time for Jim to get used to the quiet in his house. When he hears a noise from outside, it won't be from Spike. It will only be the wind or a tree branch touching the side of his house. He'll know that but he'll remember the days when a scratch on the back door told him to open it. Spike was ready to come home.

Stick That Gum Behind Your Ear

Remember when you were a kid and your teacher caught you chewing gum in class? Remember how you felt when she told you to stick the gum either on your nose or behind your ear? Without a moment's hesitation, you obediently wadded your favorite Wrigley's flavor and stuck in on your nose until it fell off. Then you picked it up and stuck it behind your ear. There it remained until the end of the school day. If your hair was long you had some explaining to do when you got home and your mother saw you trying to disentangle the gum. She saved you the trouble by cutting it out and taking a chunk of hair with it.

Can you imagine any teacher in today's school system telling a kid to stick his gum on his nose? The student would immediately get out his smartphone and ask the teacher to repeat her request. If she complied, the kid would post the video on all social media sites. The principal would see it and run down the hall to the classroom. He would fire the teacher, ask her to hand over her keys and clean out her desk. All of this, of course, would be recorded and go viral. Within an hour, the teacher's career would be over unless she was offered a job at one of Detroit's inner city schools. No gum problems there. Only firearms.

Ah, the good old days when teachers had authority over every child in the classroom and obedience was the rule instead of the exception. Some teachers made us shudder with fright. Others made us tremble at the mere thought of being called upon to stand and read aloud. A few made us feel good about our lopsided drawings during art class. While fellow students laughed at us, our music teacher might have praised our feeble attempts at getting something other than squeaks from our clarinet.

When I think back to my school days, I recall one or two teachers who were kind and showed compassion to kids having trouble with art, music, long division, or antonyms. If I dig way back in my memory, I'm sure I'll remember feeling warm and fuzzy when a teacher wrote "good" on my paper. If a gold star appeared next to a well-written sentence, I'm almost positive I floated on air for the rest of the day. However, a few memories of sheer terror remain in my mind. After all these years, I'm still trying to figure out how anything as innocent as a stick of Wrigley's Spearmint Gum could humiliate us and bring us to our knees. It was just chewing gum. It wasn't anything subversive or dangerous. It didn't take away from our concentration on geography or the Weekly Reader. It didn't fill our mouth with sweet juices like Bazooka did. True, we loved Bazooka Joe and his jokes, but we didn't dare blow bubbles in class. And finally, most of us had no idea how to make gum pop and snap when we chewed, so noise wasn't a contributing factor to our insubordination.

Why, then, were teachers so adamant about "no gum" rules in our classrooms? We were obedient little souls and never disrespected them because we feared them. With very few exceptions, they had no reason to pick on us except for a gum offense. If we knew our teacher was in a sour mood, the boys who dared chew a stick of Juicy Fruit quickly swallowed it or rolled it into a ball and stuck it underneath their desks. Chewing gum was a greater offense than hitting a kid with a snowball filled with a chunk of ice. The injured kid might have a trickle of blood running down his cheek, but the thrower got in less trouble than the kid who chewed gum in class.

I know many changes have occurred in the classroom since I was young. Although I have no evidence to support my claim, I'm willing to bet that gum is no longer considered the number one enemy of the teacher and has found its rightful place in schools if for no other reason than it's a lot safer than those expensive cell phones recording every movement of every teacher every day.

Real Women Wear Plaid

A plaid shirt is as much a part of my wardrobe today as it was when I was a kid. Some readers might remember the plaid shirts that matched the plaid lining in our overalls. Such garments were staples for kids in the 1950s. We rolled up our pant leg to show off the plaid lining. You could say we were following a trend, but in those days all we knew was that our mother had bought us a new pair of overalls.

Today I refer to my wardrobe as pathetic because it takes up about fifteen inches in my closet. With the exception of two winter jackets, I can throw every piece of clothing I own into a small garbage bag. If I spend the night at a friend's house, I toss a few essentials into a plastic Walmart bag. It wouldn't occur to me to pack a regular suitcase when a plastic bag serves the same purpose and is a lot easier to carry.

My fondness for plaid is genetic. Aunt Marie's favorite slacks were plaid green polyester with an elastic waistband. I'm not sure what year she made them, but it was probably sometime during the 1940s. The slacks wore like iron and in 1991 she was still wearing them, although they were a little shiny. Mom always wore one of Dad's plaid shirts. I still find remnants of old shirts hanging on nails in the garage or the wellhouse. The other day I came across a child's plaid shirt that belonged to one of us kids. In the old photos, someone is always wearing plaid.

There's something inherently inviting in this fabric that makes it irresistible. Maybe it's the variety of colors or the size of the squares I find attractive. Maybe it's family tradition. Everybody who was part of my childhood wore plaid. Living in the Upper Peninsula dictated a warm flannel shirt was worn at least eleven months of the year. Plaid was a natural choice for shirts with long sleeves.

If you've ever been in the military you know what they say about the summer and winter uniforms. In summer, the sleeves on shirts are rolled up. In winter, they're rolled down and buttoned. Well, it was like that around our house. Global warming had not yet reached the sideroad so most summer days demanded a warm shirt. I don't recall any kind other than flannel. A July morning bike ride required more than a thin blouse, thus the plaid shirt over it. By afternoon, the shirt might have been abandoned, but it was called back into service by early evening.

And plaid didn't stop at shirts and overalls. We had plaid blankets from Traverse Bay Woolen Company, plaid flannel nightgowns and sheets from Wards, plaid tablecloths from Cowan's Department Store, plaid socks from Ely Andary & Sons, and my dolls wore plaid dresses from Scotts Five & Dime. All these establishments are gone now, but there was a time when our downtown had a variety of clothing stores, many privately owned by local residents.

I still love plaid. I can't help it. I've tried to introduce solid-colored shirts into my closet, but the plaid always takes over and shoves the newcomers to the floor. I don't know how it happens, but a new white or pink or purple blouse is always falling off a hanger or pushed to the far corner where I don't notice it until my spring weeding. I can't stand more than a few things in my closet, so you can pretty much guess which blouses land in the give-away bag. Some solid shirts still have price tags attached. When plaid is in your blood, there's no transfusion going to cure you.

Remember the Quinlan Quints from the Canadian show "This Hour Has 22 Minutes?" The Quints were four "guys" who wore red plaid shirts and spoke Canadian. You know what I mean, eh? When I was working on my never-completed online PhD, my mentor was a fellow from Nova Scotia. His surname was Quinlan. Naturally we got to talking about "22 Minutes." I mentioned my theory that real women wear plaid. When I met him at a Minneapolis residency a few summers later, I was wearing a plaid shirt. It wasn't planned. Everything I packed was plaid, and yes, I packed a real suitcase instead of a black plastic bag. Although I'm a true Yooper, I know how to act civilized if I don't have to put on the dog for longer than a week.

Well anyway, my mentor took one look at my shirt and laughed. He said something like, "you really do wear plaid" and without hesitation I admitted I never left home without something plaid on my person. I draw the line at plaid tennis shoes, though, and plaid trousers are another nixed item. I owned a pair when I was in the eighth grade. I remember them as the ugliest things known to man or beast. Well, maybe they weren't as ugly as men's plaid leisure suits of the 1970s, but they were a close second.

So there you have it. Some obsessions last a few minutes, others a lifetime. My advice to gals is wear your plaid shirts with pride, knowing it takes a real woman to pull off plaid and still look feminine.

Farewell Old Mitts

I was taking a batch of blueberry muffins out of the oven one morning when the heat from the muffin tin went right through my oven mitts. As they age, they wear thin in the fingertip area. Since they're interchangeable, I switch from one hand to the other, but eventually the fabric gives way. That's when I know it's time to lay Old Mitts to rest.

Parting with my autumn-themed mitts is like parting with an old friend. Four years ago, I bought the mitts and hung them on hooks stuck to the side of my refrigerator. They were always available for work. They never complained about the oven's heat. They didn't grumble when it was December and they should have been replaced by the holiday-themed ones in a kitchen drawer. When winter gave way to spring, they waited for the sunflower mitts to take over, but their wait was in vain.

It was with a sigh of nostalgia I retired my orange mitts decorated with pumpkins and acorn squash. They served me well, but they're worn out and I can't trust them. I never know when my fingers will find the soft spots, and I'll feel the intense heat from a muffin tin or casserole dish. It's an awful thing when trust between good buddies comes to an end.

Why do I call a pair of oven mitts my buddies? Well, it's like this. I talk to inanimate objects. It's a habit I developed as a child when my best friends were dolls. Seventy years ago, every little girl talked to her dolls just like every little boy talked to his plastic soldiers. It was a method of learning how to converse with others even if they weren't real. Without realizing it, we were honing our conversational skills and preparing for contact with the world outside our playroom. Some youngsters discarded the habit during their teen years, but others, like myself, kept at it until our skill was perfected to an artform.

I talk to everything. It's not because I'm alone or senile. It's because I appreciate my surroundings. I praise the books on my shelves and apologize for not reading them because their print is too small. I tell the pictures on my walls we've been friends all my life, and I hope they find a good home when I'm gone. I thank the ferns in my front yard for hiding decaying tree stumps. I ask my garage roof not to collapse from the weight of snow. I caution wild rabbits feeding on clover in my yard to be aware of predators.

It's only natural I bid Old Mitts a fond farewell as I toss them in the trash. Not a glorified ending, I'll admit, but a necessary one.

When Your Dental Floss Gets Stuck

Dental floss is a great invention and so are those little plastic sticks we use to scrape plaque from our teeth. But like many inventions that didn't make it off the inventor's floor, floss and sticks also have kinks that occasionally must be dealt with. We've all experienced the frustration of floss shredding while we use it. Either it shreds or it's so thick it refuses to release once we've managed to squeeze it between our teeth. Some dental floss has the consistency of thread and other brands are more like binder twine. Lucky is the person who happens upon one that does the job without creating more trouble than it's worth.

I'll move on to the plastic sticks. I've yet to find one that isn't the equivalent of a miniature sword. One end has the potential of drawing blood if we're not careful. The opposite end has a tendency to get stuck between our teeth. Just the other evening I reached for scissors to cut through the stick that was stuck in my mouth. Luckily, my oral cavity was large enough to accommodate both stick and scissors. I opened wide and snipped the stuck stick. Perhaps you've never had the opportunity to perform this minor procedure. Consider yourself fortunate.

Years ago I used a toothbrush that came with a little rubber tip at the end of the handle. I asked Google if it had a name and discovered such low-tech instruments are still available and called "gum stimulators." It never occurred to me that gums needed stimulating, but I suppose such a maneuver helps prevent periodontal disease. Check out the Sunstar GUM 407. For less than $4 this rubber tipped, latex-free, miracle plastic toothbrush is the perfect "stimulator for gingival massage" or so says their ad. Little did I know the toothbrush I used as a kid was capable of such a marvelous feat.

Dental floss that shreds and sharp sticks that draw blood from our gums pale in the face of major problems facing us today, but there's not much we can do about climate change or the social unrest in our country. The concerns we have are closer to home, specifically in our bathroom. They're challenges we face every night when we give our teeth a final flossing and brushing. Good luck to everyone who still retains their own choppers instead of store-bought ones. The effort to keep them in good shape really is worth the trouble.

The Million Mile March of Red Squirrels

For years the red squirrels in my yard outsmarted me. No matter how hard I tried to outwit them, they always managed to cling to a birdfeeder. I tried everything. I bought feeders the size of a baseball. I was convinced they would hold no attraction for the squirrels, but I was wrong. They didn't care if they had to hang upside down or twist themselves inside out. They always managed to devour sunflower seeds meant for the chickadees.

Over the years, I invested a small fortune in feeders guaranteed to discourage or deter squirrels. I should have spent the money on a trip to Alcatraz for all the good it did. Regardless of the size or shape, squirrels found a way to gobble up the seeds and chase away the birds. I wrapped old stove pipes around the base of the trees. This didn't solve the problem. I couldn't ring all the trees with pipes, so I stood by and watched as squirrels laughed and jumped from one spruce to the next until they reached their destination.

Every year I vowed not to spend another cent on birdseed. I didn't mind buying suet because the squirrels didn't eat it, and I bought the good stuff. Real beef fat from Four Seasons Market in Brimley, not the prepackaged squares sold in stores. That stuff lasts forever. But every year I caved in when I saw chickadees and nuthatches looking for a free meal and last year was no different. I wish my heart was as cold as a steel pole, but it's not. It's soft as spun sugar so, of course, I drove to Tractor Supply and loaded the back of my vehicle with oiled sunflower seeds.

But by spring my patience had run out. For the first couple months of winter, only a few red squirrels showed up, but word soon got around and early one March morning I awoke to the sound of a family chatting outside my bedroom window. The squirrels had invited their entire clans to join them. The chickadees didn't stand a chance. Even blue jays and evening grosbeaks were chased away. Sparrows and finches didn't bother to stop. I finally had to admit I was beaten. To save myself a mountain of stress, it was time to put the feeders in the garage and call it quits. My solution lasted only a few hours. I felt sorry for the chickadees as they landed on familiar limbs looking for their breakfast. I put out another chunk of suet and that gesture temporarily eased my guilt, but I knew I had to do more. Where could I hang the feeders so the squirrels couldn't reach them? Nowhere, as far as I could figure. Then out of the blue a brilliant idea struck. What about my clothesline?

Immediately I put on my boots, jacket, scarf, hat, and gloves and headed for the garage. I filled a feeder, found some clothes-pins and a short bungee cord. I tramped out to the clothesline hung between two cedar poles. I wrapped the cord around the feeder's chain and then around the line. I secured it with the clothespins and presto, my squirrel problem was solved.

Although they could run up the poles, they couldn't walk the tightrope clothesline. No trees were close enough for them to fly through the air so there was no way for them to reach their goal. The line was too high for jumping, and they couldn't figure out how to form a squirrel pyramid. And they weren't strong enough to drag the ladder from the garage and lean it against the feeder.

Ah, sweet success. I had finally outsmarted the squirrels. The next day I hung another feeder and watched as chickadees zoomed in. Sunflower seeds lasted a lot longer when they weren't raided by squirrels. When I looked out my kitchen window I missed seeing all the activity because the clothesline was a good distance away, but I was content knowing chickadees, nuthatches, and sparrows would have plenty to eat as winter wound down.

The answer to my dilemma had been there all along, staring me straight in the face. Every day as I walked past the clothesline to scatter cracked corn for my partridges I saw that line, but I didn't see it as a solution. Then my only worry was the Million Mile March of Red Squirrels as they plotted their revenge. I visualized it in my mind. A million red squirrels convening in my backyard, each complaining that their food source had disappeared and each suggesting how they could force me to put feeders within their reach.

They also knew the seeds were kept in the garage, the same place where they had chewed the lining from old rubber boots and the shelves of an even older pie safe. They had chewed through a plastic garbage can filled with seeds. They had knocked various items to the cement floor. By the end of April, I was so tired of finding seeds in every corner of my garage and underneath the glove box in my car, I decided I would never again feed anything when winter rolled around. The birds would be on their own, and it was all because of red squirrels. If anyone feels sorry for these pests, a few are still hanging around my yard. Feel free to drive over and take them home. No questions asked.

The Thursday Night Bellyache

One cold winter morning, I was chatting on the telephone with my brother when the conversation unexpectedly turned to something he referred to as the Thursday Night Bellyache. I asked if it was a new malady raging across the country. Was it something mentioned on the Dr. Oz show? Was there a pill for it? What were my chances of catching it? Was it fatal?

My brother laughed. The gist of what he said went like this. When a kid doesn't want to go to school on Friday, he doesn't wait until the morning to begin his act. He starts rehearsing Thursday evening. He holds his belly and tells Mother he isn't feeling well. She puts her hand on his forehead which does seem a little warm. She fills a glass with tepid water, drops an Alka-Seltzer into it, and hands it to him.

At this point, Junior has two options. He can down the awful-tasting stuff or he can fess up. Naturally, the kid has no intention of telling the truth. He drinks the fizzy medicine, burps a few times and waits. Meanwhile Mother has moved on to more pressing issues like ironing his best shirt for the next day. She is well acquainted with the routine because it happens almost every Thursday night. Junior doesn't hate school. He hates his teacher because she picks on him.

By morning, Junior's bellyache has morphed into a blazing BELLYACHE. He's convinced himself he's also suffering from a raging fever and no amount of reassurance by Mother can change his mind. His forehead does seem warmer than usual and his tears appear genuine. Mother is torn between sending a sick child to school or falling for his performance. She ponders which decision will cause her the least amount of trouble. She reasons he can make up the spelling test on Monday if he really is sick. And if he's faking an illness, it's still more prudent to err on the side of caution.

Junior gets a hug from Mother. The second she leaves his room he snuggles underneath the covers, congratulates himself on a job well done, and drifts off to dreamland. That, in a very long nutshell, is the definition of the Thursday Night Bellyache. Some readers might recall the days of their youth when fear of being picked on by a teacher or a classroom bully forced them to feign a bellyache to temporarily avoid the dreaded schoolhouse.

Our conversation got me thinking about Christmas. A few days before the 25th I asked my friend, Tony, to accompany me when I made the rounds delivering cookies to older friends. I said it would be nice to visit them because they don't get out very often. They look forward to and appreciate company. My friend agreed it was a good idea. Through many years of sabotaging his relationships until they became defunct, he had learned that saying YES at the first request saved the inevitable squabbling that resulted if he immediately said NO. He also learned to bide his time. By six o'clock on the evening of the 23rd he called and said he was getting the sniffles. I extended my condolences and suggested he drop an Alka-Seltzer into a glass of warm water.

He called back at 8:00 p.m. and said the sniffles had become a full-blown cold. I told him to rub Vicks on his chest, warm a flannel rag, and place it over the Vicks to accelerate the healing. Such a remedy always worked when I was a kid. If it had no effect, I suggested he get out the Musterole, a medicinal rub he had never heard of, so that remedy was not a good alternative.

As I hung up the phone it occurred to me Tony was pulling his version of the Thursday Night Bellyache. The ache had simply moved from his belly to his nose. When the phone rang the next morning, I didn't need caller I.D. to know who was on the other end. With all the self-confidence of a well-trained actor, the weak voice, nasal tone, and intermittent cough assured me Tony was going nowhere. He was staying in bed with his affliction. I wished him a speedy recovery and went on my way.

Come the dawn of Christmas morn, Tony called and said all his symptoms had disappeared. By noon he was standing at my front door looking robust and healthy. All signs of a cold had vanished as quickly as they had come. He was eager for lunch and a little gambling at the casino. After a hardy meal and a few unsuccessful turns at the slots, he returned home a happy man.

Which only goes to show, the Thursday Night Bellyache is a temporary ailment guaranteed to turn Friday or any other day into a very pleasant one. Being a woman of pristine character, it's a stunt I haven't pulled, but I understand why it comes easily to fellows. Whether a kid or a man, sometimes it's easier to lie than tell the truth and face an argument. If a child has a bellyache due to fear, it's understandable he wants to stay home. If a man agrees to accompany you on an outing but then falls ill, he avoids the predictable bickering that results from his change of mind. After all, no one is to blame for catching a cold.

Thinking back over the years and all the tiffs I've created by telling the truth, perhaps I should have conjured up something as ridiculous as the Thursday Night Bellyache and saved myself a whole lot of aggravation. And if I had purchased stock in Vicks VapoRub, Musterole, or Alka-Seltzer, I might be a wealthy woman today. Of course, like most shows the bellyache act is only good for a certain number of performances. If used too often, parents and friends get wise to the shenanigans and like it or not, the jig's up. Eventually the youngster accepts his fate and his belly gets better as he gets braver and school is not so scary. And what happens to the friend with the one-day sniffles? Well, I guess that depends upon your level of tolerance for baloney.

There Was a Time

There was a time a long time ago when women stayed home and ran the household. They cared for the children, cooked and cleaned, did the washing and ironing, baked the bread, and tried to please everyone. The generations of Mom and Gram and multiple generations of women before them worked from first light until the kerosene lamp gave out, the wood in the kitchen stove burned to embers, and their day finally ended. Such women kept their complaints to themselves. Their daily lives were filled with toil. I imagine their nights were filled with anxiety about their family, finances, and the farm.

What happened to such women? Are they all gone now? Have they passed away as quietly and softly as morning dew? What legacy did they leave? I remember my mother's hands. They were strong yet gentle like the rest of her. Mom was the same as many other women. Work was her occupation. Whether in the house or at the barn, work was all she knew. Her reprieve came for an hour on Sunday mornings when she dressed in her best clothes and attended church. When she returned home, her good clothes were hung on hangers, an apron was put over her housedress, and the daily routine continued. Mom never could have guessed that in years to come very few women would assume the roles once reserved for women throughout the ages. She knew her role of housewife and mother would mimic that of her mother. She knew what was expected of her, just as Dad knew his role as husband and father. The lines never blurred. Each had an example set by their parents. My maternal grandmother passed away before I was born, but she taught Mom well. My paternal grandfather passed when Dad was ten years old, yet somehow Dad knew he was the provider and protector of his family.

Throughout history, there have been women who shunned lives of drudgery, but they are few in number compared to the women who accepted the yoke of traditional womanhood. It was a comfort knowing Mom was always home. We took her for granted. When her sister, Kate, was dying from cancer, Mom spent most of one year caring for her. The house was often cold when we got home from school. Dad was at work, Gram had moved to town, and there was no one to keep the kitchen woodstove going. I dreaded coming home to a cold, empty house. Home wasn't home without Mom. She's been gone for many years, but I still miss her and treasure her memory and the days when she was nearby whenever I needed her. She was a steady rock in rough waters. An inspiration in times of hopelessness and my strength when I was weak. She was my faithful, loving Mother.

Embracing the Crow's Foot

My first sewing experience was using Mom's old treadle machine. As some women will remember, we were given a piece of notebook paper and told to follow the lines. Sounds like an easy assignment, right? Wrong. For fellows who are laughing, I challenge you. Ask your wife or girlfriend for a piece of lined paper, sit at her sewing machine, and try to follow the lines without zigzagging all over the paper. Then tell me how much success you had. And, please, do not thread the needle or you'll land in big trouble.

Home Economics used to be a basic course in a public school curriculum. In Brimley, seventh grade was the year girls were taught to sew. Our teacher handed out sheets of paper with lines on them. Once we mastered straight lines, we were given sheets with circles, triangles, and other geometric shapes. Some of us learned quickly because we had practiced at home. After we had proven our ability to navigate intricate maneuvers required when sewing a complex pattern, we were allowed to tackle thread and cloth.

But a true seamstress knows there's more to sewing than just creating straight seams, precise gathers, and perfectly set-in sleeves. Finer details must be considered. Making bound buttonholes is one of them. Covering metal buttons with material that matches the garment is another. Selecting buttons that lend flair to the finished item is a third detail highlighting the creativity of the seamstress.

Almost anyone can sew a button on a shirt. Most females have a natural ability for it. Some fellows learned while sailing on a Great Lakes Freighter. Others learned when in the military. Many more learned out of sheer desperation when a button fell off their shirt moments before attending an important event. However, there's more to attaching a button than merely poking a needle in and out of the holes. There's the Crow's Foot.

Often referred to as "fleur de lis" by the French, the stitch symbolizes the king's divinity. Although not difficult, it is a bit complicated and requires patience to sew it properly. You won't find the stitch on mass-produced clothing purchased from Walmart or any other store unless money is no object, in which case a trip to Harrods in London or Brown-Thomas in Dublin is in the cards. It's a clever person, usually a woman, who will hone her sewing skills on something as simple and overlooked as a button. How many times have you examined the buttons holding your shirts and pants together? Probably never, but I'll bet at this very moment you're Googling the stitch to see what it looks like because you won't find it on your mass-produced clothing. However, you may have found a new appreciation for that little plastic button on your shirt or pants that keeps your chest or belly from popping out like a jack-in-the-box.

Mending the Holes in My Jeans

The other day I was talking to a friend and he told me I was in style because my jeans were ripped and my right knee was exposed. I explained that as a creature of habit, I had been wearing the jeans almost every day for three years. I agreed the denim was getting a bit thin in the knee area. A few days previous to my friend's observation, I noticed a small rip but ignored it until I put my foot through it while pulling on the jeans one morning in my dark bedroom.

During my two-year garage sale purge, I sold my sewing machine and everything that went with it including a decorative canister filled with buttons, dozens of spools of thread, various size needles, snaps, hooks, scissors, pinking shears, patterns, fabric, and all the other essentials a seamstress needs to set up shop. However, in case of an emergency I did keep a needle and two spools of thread—one white, one black.

The evening of the day when I could no longer ignore the rip that grew larger with the passing of each hour, I got out the black thread with the needle stuck in it. My eyesight is not the best and the needle's hole was tiny but after a few stabs I managed to push the thread through the eye. I hadn't patched anything in years, but it took only a minute to fold one piece of fabric over the other and close the rip with a simple blind stitch I learned in the seventh grade.

Those were the days when home economics was a required course. Making a skirt was our first major sewing machine project after we had mastered the ability to sew a straight line without running the machine's needle over our fingers. Some of my classmates might remember we were not allowed to put a zipper in the skirt. Instead, we sewed little snaps where the zipper would have gone and used a hook and eye on the band for the closure. Our Home Economics teacher insisted we learn the old-fashioned way of making do with what we had. Zippers were for rich people. Snaps were for country folks. Hooks and eyes were cheap.

We were also taught multiple methods of blind stitching. Since I knew my jeans would eventually land in the rag bag, I chose the easiest one called the running stitch. When I reached the end of the rip, there was ample thread left on the needle so I did a simple cross stitch. Now my worn-out jeans look almost like new. As a neighbor remarked when he saw my handiwork, "There's still a lot of wear left in 'em."

What he said made sense. There is wear left in just about everything we own, but instead of "making do" we run to the nearest store or online site and buy something new. We love to shop and discard jeans or shirts or cars or anything that's beginning to show its age. Perhaps that's why so many marriages fall apart after a few years. Now don't get excited if you've just filed for divorce because your wife gained a few pounds or your husband bought another rifle. Think about what you're trading in for a newer model. It might not be worth the trouble.

The Plastic Tomato Experiment

Six weeks ago I bought four tomatoes from a local grocery store. They were clustered on the vine and their stickers said they were grown in Canada. I felt good knowing they hadn't traveled thousands of miles to reach the store's shelf. Although the exact location wasn't mentioned, Canada is a lot closer to Michigan than Mexico or China. I had faith the tomatoes might have some taste. The first thing I did when I got home was make a lettuce and tomato sandwich. It was delicious.

Within a few days, all the tomatoes had been consumed except one. I left it on the kitchen counter. I guess you might say I had decided to conduct a non-scientific experiment. My counter was the laboratory. The tomato was the specimen. I was waiting for it to show signs of decay.

Other than some slight shriveling around the stem end, by the second week it remained firm to the touch and gave no indication it was past its prime. After five weeks, I was quickly losing faith that my bright red Canadian fruit was preferable to any grown in my own country. For some unknown reason, I thought Canadian growers used fewer toxins on their crops than we do. Apparently I was wrong.

There's no earthly reason why a tomato should last six weeks on my counter and not spoil unless, of course, it's been doused with a cocktail of pesticides. I'm thoroughly disappointed in the Canadians, and I won't be making another purchase from them no matter how inviting their tomatoes look. We all know you can't judge a book by its cover. By now I should know I can't judge fruit by its enticing appearance. Just like good-looking people, good-looking fruit is often deceiving.

When I eventually sliced the tomato to see if it was rotting from within, it was perfect. It reminded me of the portrait of Dorian Gray. Neither he nor my tomato showed any signs of age. I hesitated to taste it, although I figured my chances of survival were good. I took one nibble and that was enough. It was totally tasteless and as harmless as chewing on a piece of cardboard.

I thought back to the day when I had purchased the tomatoes. They were not overly ripe, just the way I like them. Then I thought about the sandwiches I'd made with salt, pepper, and Miracle Whip. I began to wonder if these, plus the lettuce, were responsible for the great tasting sandwich. Perhaps my beautiful red fruit had been tasteless from the beginning. By adding seasonings and salad dressing, I was fooled into thinking the tomato was delicious. Discovering the truth was kind of like a husband seeing his beautiful bride after she removes her makeup, her false eyelashes, and her hair extensions— almost frightening and, perhaps, a downright disappointment.

Thoughts on Mice and Lice

Remember when a mouse was something you caught in a trap and didn't want to touch? When I was a kid, checking Mom's mouse trap line was my least favorite chore. I didn't mind dust-mopping the bedroom floors because I listened to the hit parade on the radio and sang along with the week's top twenty records. It took me an hour to dust the upstairs when it was only a fifteen-minute job. Mom knew I squandered as much time as possible because I dreaded my worst afternoon chore. Checking Mom's trap line was anathema to me, especially when the mouse's beady black eyes stared into mine.

Mom's favorite place to set traps was the pantry. Our pantry wasn't just a closet with shelves like you might find in today's modern, sophisticated homes. It was a small room with a pie safe, a wooden table, and plenty of storage boxes nailed to the wall. The pie safe held our spices, canned goods, cookie sheets, good dishes, pots, and frying pans. I don't recall a pie ever being placed in there because a pie never lasted long enough to be stored anywhere.

Our farmhouse was typical of most. There were lots of places where mice could squeeze through and look for winter lodging. We were luckier than our neighbors. Rarely did a rodent venture near the pantry and never did one enter our living quarters. One of my lady friends is always finding a dead mouse in her shoe or underneath her bed or a live one nibbling some delicacy on her kitchen counter. Her cat gets his daily exercise and entertainment by chasing mice, pouncing on them, and slapping them with his paws. When he gets bored, he eats them.

In today's society, having a rodent in the house is a common occurrence. Some parents actually buy mice and rats as pets for their children, a phenomenon beyond my understanding. Years ago housewives were embarrassed if they saw a furry gray thing scurry across the room. This was especially true if company had stopped by for morning coffee. No one wanted to admit a mouse was on the loose in their kitchen, and heaven forbid if something was heard running through the rafters. Today's kids proudly display their collection of rodents, and some parents let them wander at will throughout the entire premises.

It's the same with lice. In my day, people were horrified if their kid came home scratching his head, but in our shiny new century, lice seem to be accepted as a normal part of grade school. This amazes me. When and why did we get so complacent about things as repulsive as mice and lice? My reaction to these pests borders on phobic, but that's how I was raised. Rodents were not allowed in the house, and lice were a scourge forbidden near our heads.

Throughout grade school, I recall only one louse episode in our school. The infected kids stayed home until all signs of nits were kerosened out of their heads. I remember feeling sorry for the children. Mom explained it wasn't their fault, and we shouldn't mention it to anyone. People were easily humiliated in those days. An outbreak of lice was unthinkable. Today it's as natural as a recess break.

Anyway, when I checked Mom's trap line and found a mouse, I didn't care that it was dead. It didn't belong in the house so it got what it deserved. It wasn't the lifeless rodent that bothered me. It was the idea of touching a furry dead thing. I could swat a fly or squish a mosquito on my arm and think nothing of it, but no way would I remove a mouse from a trap. Likewise, Dad and my siblings wouldn't go near the thing either, but it didn't bother Mom. She was our hero.

Fast forward to today. With all the words available, it's amazing that "mouse" is the best techies could come up with to describe the little black thing I maneuver with my right hand every time I use my computer. I'd be lost without my mouse. Words I never dreamed would tumble from my mouth.

My Sleepwear Lost Its Flannel

Last fall I purchased a new flannel nightgown. It helped warm me during the long winter nights and was soft to the touch. Soon the weather should be mild enough to give the gown its last washing prior to retiring it for the summer. In previous years, I've taken the flannel sheets off my bed and removed my electric blanket. I've put away my winter bathrobe and nightgowns. Then the middle of May rolls around with close to freezing temperatures. This year I'm taking no chances. Everything's staying put until July.

That's the good news. Here's the bad. Every time I washed my new sleepwear, it lost more of its flannel. I know one more spin in the washing machine and a quick tumble in the dryer and the remainder of the flannel will be gone. I'll be left with a rough, scratchy material to match my flannel-less flannel sheets. This was the second year for the sheet set. It might be the last. Ditto for my new nightgown.

The problem isn't the bedding or the sleepwear. Nor is it the dryer. The culprit gobbling the flannel is my energy-efficient washing machine. Because it uses only a teaspoon of water per load, the fibers have no choice but to rub against each other. The friction they create robs the cotton of its outer layer. The highly efficient washing machines of today are efficient in only one area. They destroy clothing. The front loaders use much less water than their top loading counterparts, but they're responsible for the deterioration of whatever is being washed in them.

Prior to purchasing the new machine, I used an old one that demanded as much water as a traveler crossing the Sahara. For years I put my clothing and bedding in water-guzzling monsters. Sheets, towels, and clothing came out of the washer and dryer as soft as they went in. Socks might have been eaten, but no washer ever took a bite out of the heels. Sweaters might have shrunk, maybe even pilled, but their fibers retained the original texture. Washcloths did not feel like steel wool.

Maybe this is the new normal. Maybe I keep items long past their prime. Perhaps I should toss things out and stop expecting them to last five years as they used to. Perhaps I should be contributing more to the economy instead of bemoaning the short life-expectancy of washables. Well, I don't know. In many ways, this new century continues to mystify me. Things supposed to make our life easier seem to add more frustration than ease. A washing machine that destroys clothing is just one example of how far modern technology has taken us and how little benefit we've gained from it.

An energy efficient toilet is another example of energy efficiency gone awry. True, it uses much less water than the old kind, but it also requires three flushes. If you have one of these modern marvels, you know what I mean. Thankfully, I'm still clinging to my old toilet. It will take an act of Congress to pry it loose from me.

And so it goes. From flannel to flushing, the old ways are passing.

Get Your Snowball Scoop Today

Black Friday is here. Well, actually, it's been here for most of the month. Shopping channels offering free shipping and mailboxes full of catalogs are testimony to the frantic push to buy, buy, buy. Shoppers have been a bit on the lazy side and retailers are doing their best to stay afloat. Sometimes I toss the catalogs into the recycling bin, but occasionally I look at them. That's what boredom will do to a person.

While thumbing through the Lakeside Catalog, I noticed an item that reminded me of the old days when we did things the hard way. You remember those days. Every Monday our mother washed clothes in a wringer washing machine. Every Saturday night we bathed in a granite tub. We drank milk that came straight from the cows in our barn. Instead of using a machine to blow away autumn leaves, we raked them. And when winter deposited its bounty, we made snowballs by grabbing handfuls of the white stuff and shaping them into spheres.

So when I saw an ad for a snowball scoop, I realized the time had come for me to write a book titled, "Snowball Making for Dummies." Such a name might impinge upon copyright laws, but that's a minor detail to be worked out in the future by a lawyer. For now, all I have is the idea because the old technique of creating snowballs has apparently disappeared along with the old way of washing clothes, taking baths, drinking milk, and raking leaves.

The plastic snowball maker looked like two ice cream scoops facing each other. They were held together by one screw. The ad was a little short on directions, but I'm sure it wouldn't take long for kids to figure out how to use it. I'm only guessing, but I think snow would have to be the right consistency to eliminate any possibility of releasing the ball from the plastic gizmo without breaking it or the snowball.

I can picture it now. Johnny and Jane are dressed in their warmest winter garb. Their mother hands them a red or blue snowball scoop and tells them to go outside and play. The kids might wonder what "play" means and why they need a scoop, but they won't question their mother or such a marvelous piece of modern equipment. They might get a little frustrated when the snowball won't release or the snow is too soft and melts before becoming a ball. They might even cry tears of frustration when the snow is too crusty and the scoop cracks, rendering their colorful new tool useless.

But there's always hope an adult would come along and comfort the kids. I have a feeling the first thing he would do is dig a hole, bury the scoop, grab a handful of snow and make the perfect ball. Then before running back to their bedrooms and digital devices, Johnny and Jane would probably agree to pelt any adult who ever again offered them a plastic snowball maker.

Part IV:
Sundry Rambles

One Man's Junk

We've all heard the expression "one man's junk is another man's treasure" and it was never so true as when I contacted a handyman for his opinion on a roof repair job. I had some trees taken down that were too near an old playhouse. Once they were removed, problems became apparent. The way I saw it, the roofing was coming off exposing the wood beneath it. I thought adhering another piece of roofing material would be a temporary way to keep out the weather, which only goes to show I know nothing about anything.

The solution suggested by the "handyman" who had become an "expert" was to tear down the building. I agreed the roof did look in rough condition and the building was a bit shabby. I agreed there wasn't much of a foundation and the window was broken. I said there wasn't anything of value in the structure, at least nothing of monetary value. Then I thought about all the time, energy, and love that had gone into what had once been a child's playhouse.

I thanked the man for his time. He handed me his card and said if I ever had a "real" job for him, he might consider it. He was very busy with big projects that brought in real money. When he drove away, I returned to the playhouse and tried to figure out how I could fix the damage. After dismissing a number of ideas I didn't think would work, I did what a lot of women my age would have done in a similar situation. I sat on a bench and cried.

What the man had seen as junk, I saw as easily repairable with a small amount of cost and effort. Silly me. I forgot we live in a throw-away world. There's no point in trying to save something when it's much easier to tear it down, burn the lumber, and rebuild a $20,000 playhouse that will never be seen by anyone and will never be played in by the children who are now grown and have children of their own who have no interest in a homemade playhouse. I forgot that emotional attachments to anything old is often viewed as an unhealthy response to change in today's sophisticated society.

But I'm an old burr. Although the playhouse roof needs repair, I'll cling to the hope that it will survive the winter and eventually I'll find someone next spring willing to fix it. When every nail has been pounded in place by a father who made something special for his children, I think the building deserves more than a lit match or a bulldozer. I think it deserves a second chance if only for the treasured memories it brings to the ones who played in it during their childhood and as a thank-you to the memory of the man who built it.

The PC Police and Lil' Dutch Maid

In a world gone mad over political correctness, one name continues to stand the test of time. Although the cookies she promotes do not taste the same as they did years ago, the Lil' Dutch maid has not surrendered to the PC police. Her outfit has changed, she's aged along with the rest of us, and she's clung to her maidenhood. However, you know as well as I do that if the PC fanatics get a whiff of the little maiden, trouble will come calling for the company that continues to use an archaic logo with negative connotations.

Today it's downright illegal to refer to a gal as a maid. The little Dutch girl has been around since 1924 when two brothers from the Netherlands opened a bakery in Goshen, IN. I won't go into all the details, but if you're wondering how to spend the next fifteen minutes, Google the bakery. It's an interesting story, but now back to mine. As I was saying, calling a gal a "maid" leaves nothing to the imagination. Either she was passed over by fellows and became an Old Maid or she's a hardworking charwoman.

Whichever is true, the fact that she's still called a "maid" is grounds for a protest if not an all out boycott of AbiMar Foods of Abilene, Texas who now own the company started by the brothers. How dare they plaster their bags of cookies with images of a blonde haired, blue eyed maiden in full Dutch attire complete with a Voldendam bonnet? We're almost twenty-five years into the new century. We're past the Dark Ages, the Middle Ages, and chances are good we'll never live to see the Age of Aquarius.

The original owners of the bakery died years ago. I have no idea if their descendants resent the depiction of a Dutch maiden on the package or if they love it. Tradition is a wonderful thing when it's a good tradition, but not so good if it brings pain. Being drawn and quartered is not a good thing. The guillotine is not a good thing. Consuming Almond Windmills or Coconut Bars is not a good thing if we eat the entire contents of the bag in one go. It's a delightful thing when dunking only a few cookies in a glass of cold milk or a cup of hot tea.

You probably think what got me thinking about cookies was the bag of Windmills on my kitchen table. I could lie and say you're mistaken, but lying is not a good idea. A person needs an excellent memory to be a liar. I've always found it's much easier to tell the truth regardless of the consequences. Yes, I did buy some Windmill

Cookies with a picture of the pretty little maiden on the bag. So, hat's off to Lil' Dutch Maid. I hope the PC zealots never change you.

Expect Nothing and You Won't Be Disappointed

High expectations often leave us disappointed. For example, when a special occasion rolls around and Boyfriend or Hubby tells you to expect something amazing, you assume he's going to pop the question or buy you a new car. You rehearse your acceptance or thank you speech. You don't want to appear too eager, but neither do you want to act too nonchalant. You perfect your response by practicing it in front of the bathroom mirror. Unfortunately, when Girlfriend opens her gift it isn't an engagement ring she finds, but a pair of cheap earrings. Wifey is given a toaster.

February 14 and December 25 are probably the two most important dates on a girl's calendar. If she's been with Boyfriend for over a year, she expects the fellow to man up and slip a ring on her finger. If she's been married for forty years or more, it's time for a gift reminding her how important she is to Hubby. It's time to give her something spectacular to celebrate their many years together. A gift that reflects his increasing love for the mother of his children, his faithful companion, and the woman who won his heart.

So Wifey isn't worried when Hubby places a box the size of a toaster in front of her because she knows he's only fooling. Even the weight of the present is not a deterrent. She's well aware of his sense of humor. The box is probably full of rocks plucked from their driveway. She chuckles as she unwraps the gift and finds a toaster. She's unconcerned. She knows there's a Tiffany Celebration Diamond ring hiding somewhere among the cardboard and tissue paper. With a hopeful heart, she pushes aside the paper and cardboard until the box is empty. The gift she was expecting is nowhere to be found.

Wifey's present really is the stainless steel object before her that guarantees a golden brown toast on every slice of white bread. Hubby doesn't even notice her disappointment as he takes the present from her hands, plugs it in, and promptly sticks four slices of Bunny Bread into the slots. He produces a new jar of crabapple jelly and fiddles with the dials on the toaster. Wifey clings to the hope that she'll find a ring buried within the jelly. She sticks a spoon in the jar and stirs, but again she's disappointed.

If Hubby had kept his mouth shut about a "special" gift, she would have been happy with a toaster because they needed one. Their old Sunbeam was a wedding gift that had stopped turning bread into anything remotely resembling toast, but that's the way it goes. Sometimes people raise our expectations beyond their ability to produce. It's nobody's fault. It's just a case of misunderstood semantics.

Men aren't on the same wavelength as women. You know what I mean. We mention the porch steps need painting. Hubby buys the most expensive product on the market, the finest horsehair brushes, various size paint trays, and plastic tarps. He dresses as if going into combat. We watch in amazement as he proceeds with a two-hour task that would have taken us ten minutes. All we wanted was a quick slap of paint to cover the claw marks Ms. Kitty left when she sharpened her nails.

Men are notorious for overkill on simple things. They want the job done right while most gals just want the project completed. It takes me three seconds to make my bed. Some men struggle to make the hospital style corners they learned in boot camp. When I hang a picture, I pound a nail in the wall and hope for the best. A hired hand would get out a stud finder, yardstick, level, and an assortment of nails, screws, hammers, and drills. By the time every tool in his arsenal is assembled, I would have moved on to another project. Lowering expectations results in less disappointment. Give it a try and you'll be surprised at the pleasant and stress-free results. In other words, expect nothing and you won't be disappointed.

My Toilet Sweats

During the six months of winter, I long for warm summer days and so does my toilet. As soon as my place heats up, that white porcelain fixture can't wait to start dripping. Condensation forms on the tank and runs to the floor as fast as a kid runs for a fly ball. It's been a yearly occurrence for as long as I can remember. Soon it will be time to get out a towel and place it underneath the tank. That's one more chore added to my daily routine. Each day I replace the wet towel with a dry one. Whenever I'm in the bathroom, I swipe the condensation with a paper towel or a rag. The water in the tank is so cold it tells me who's boss without ever uttering a word.

Does your toilet demand attention during summer? Are you plagued with dripping water that you don't notice until there's a large puddle on your floor and you step in it, slip, and land on your rear end? Probably not. You're probably luckier than I am. Remember how Rodney Dangerfield complained he didn't get any respect? Well,

I might get a little respect, but I don't have much luck in the toilet department.

I realize that into every life a little rain must fall, but I prefer that it fall outside where it belongs. Years ago, the green refrigerator that came with this mobile home built up condensation on its top. I never noticed it until one day I realized water was running down the side of the fridge. I got out the stepladder and saw the top of the fridge was soaking wet. Why, I wondered? Why is the fridge sweating in such an odd place?

Well, I don't know. Eventually the fridge developed a new ailment and decided to run for twenty-four hours straight. I awoke one morning and found everything inside it frozen solid. I'm not talking about the freezer compartment. I'm talking about milk, eggs, celery, ketchup, and everything else in the "fridge" part of the refrigerator. I solved the problem by unplugging it at night. By morning everything had thawed and life was good.

I kept that old fridge on life supports until I finally admitted it was time for it to go. When the fellow delivered the new one, he complained about the weight of Old Green. I said of course it was heavy. It was made of metal instead of plastic. The chap scratched his head and said he had never heard of such a thing.

But back to my toilet. I keep a stack of rags at the ready when the temperature rises. I'm no longer fooled by that innocent-looking tank. I know what it's planning. Is yours hatching the same plan to flood your bathroom floor with an abundance of condensation? If so, you're an official member of the "My Toilet Sweats Club." Look for a bulletin inviting you to our next monthly meeting. I'll provide the sweets if you promise to bring your own rag and wipe my tank after you flush. You'll feel right at home.

A Kitchen Full of Memories

When the house of my youth was still standing, I often opened the kitchen door and stepped into the past. Every place I looked held a memory. The cook stove stood in its corner. The empty woodbox next to it gave silent testimony to the many cords of maple and birch that had once heated the room. I vaguely recalled at one time we burned coal, but I was too young to remember when or where it was stored. The water kettle remained on a burner. Like the stove, it had served its purpose and was no longer called into service. The white cupboard housed empty Peter Pan drinking jars, chipped dishes, and miss-matched salt and pepper shakers. The junk drawer was filled with broken toys, woolen mittens knitted by my grandmother, calendars from the 1950s, and bits and pieces of discarded items.

The electric clock above the kitchen table had been unplugged at 1:47 in 1968, the year my parents purchased a new mobile home and evacuated the house. A bench leaned against the west wall. A green oilcloth covered the table that was now covered with dead flies. Three wooden chairs surrounded the table. Frayed curtains hung limp from their rods. Green window shades attempted to block out the afternoon sun.

The door of our Frigidaire stood ajar. The radio atop it was gone, but in my mind's eye I could see our gray cat, Puff, as he slept on the radio. He must have jumped on the table that held our water pails and from there jumped to the top of the fridge. Cats were allowed in the house, but not on the tables. Puff would have claimed his spot during the night when he was safe from discovery. Once found in the morning, he would have been shooed down, and perched on the woodbox.

The washstand held a white granite bowl and a soap holder with a dried-up piece of Lifebuoy in it. A small metal box nailed to the wall contained combs without teeth and a few bobby pins. The medicine cabinet was empty. Tubes of various ointments, Bayer aspirins, band-aids, and other necessary medicines had been removed. The bulb in the light fixture above the stand had no current passing through it, but no one had bothered to remove the bulb. It went down with the house.

Somehow the pantry to the left of the woodstove remained as I remembered. The pie safe was filled with cans of spices, pie plates, muffin tins, candy boxes, and lots of other stuff. Large black pans for baking cinnamon rolls hung from nails on the wall. The turkey roaster was on the wooden table. Old clothing and rags were stored in bushel baskets. My maternal grandparents' trunk from Austria was hidden underneath woolen blankets. The milk separator claimed one corner. The shelves above it held empty cigar boxes. A Prince Albert tobacco tin was next to the boxes. It was a reminder of the days when men rolled their cigarettes.

Mom's aprons hung from nails. Dad's harness contraption for his back was next to them. He was always in pain from a sledding prank pulled on him by a nephew. Rag rugs covered the linoleum floor. The floor, itself, was the only one that had survived the ravages of a house with no foundation.

So ends the tour of the kitchen of my youth without mention of the chicken wallpaper, until now that is. It continued to dance around the walls, completely indifferent to the quiet surrounding it.

Celebrating a National Day of Scream

If you're like me, every now and then you just want to scream about something. It might be the price of coffee or gas. It might be the way your hair looks when you leave the beauty parlor. Maybe your kids are driving you nuts. Maybe it's the flat tire on your way to church or the fender bender you're involved in the day after your husband dropped full insurance coverage on your car. You just need a good scream to make everything go away.

It's often the little things in life that get us down. The years have taught us to expect major problems and catastrophes, and we've learned to accept and deal with them. It's the loose filling in our tooth or the wet newspaper or the pen without ink that drives us crazy. Which brings me to the point of this musing. We need a special day when we can let off steam. A day set aside to rid ourselves of pent-up stress. Twenty-four hours of uninterrupted hollering, shouting, or yelling at everything and everybody that's bothering us. Friends, family members, neighbors, strangers, pets, circumstances, or objects that rouse our temper during the year would have to endure the national holiday and not respond with so much as a word, a bark, or a meow.

Maybe it already exists. Maybe somewhere in some little town across this great country, there might be a celebration dubbed the National Day of Scream. If there isn't, we should start a grassroots campaign demanding our do-nothing Congress declares such a day. Our feeble leaders could choose a month that's a little lean on holidays. August springs to mind. Other than county fairs, it's a fairly dull month. On the chosen day, folks would be encouraged to scream as often and as long and loud as their lungs and throat could last. People from all generations, races, and religions could release all their anger, frustration, and disappointment. Everyone would have the right to scream at anyone, and no one would be allowed to take offense. We could release a cascade of tension and anxiety without fear of retaliation.

Munch's famous painting, "The Scream," has always fascinated me. Critics speculate it's a self-portrait, the result of the artist's agoraphobia. Well, I don't know any more than the critics, but I have a theory. I think Munch was at his wits' end and needed an outlet.

What better way to preserve a strong emotion than to commit it to canvas? Maybe Munch was having a bad day. Maybe one bad day rolled into another and another until the days became years and his only escape was his art and that painting.

The first time I came across Munch's anxiety paintings, I found them rather disturbing. Who would want to hang such macabre works in their living room? The very fact it's called a "living room" would negate the purchase of such art because his models do not appear to be enjoying life. In "The Scream," the screamer is holding his hands over his ears. One could argue he's tired of hearing the noise in his head so he covers his ears and emits a scream no one can hear. Isn't that the zenith of frustration? I'll give you an example.

The other day I was ready to scream at the unfairness of life. I know everything is random, but some people seem to have all the luck. They sail through life without ever having a problem. But I'll bet, just like everybody else, these lucky people could benefit from a good healthy scream. It must be difficult maintaining appearances and pretending they don't have a care or worry in the world. A loud and long scream might work wonders in liberating all the frustrations layered behind their smiles and laughter. So, there you have it. Until Congress acts, I suppose we'll have to settle for imitating Munch's famous painting. Open our mouth wide and release a silent scream. Nobody will hear it, but maybe we'll feel better knowing we initiated our own National Day of Scream.

The Potato and the Egg

I saw a post on Facebook that really hit home. It was about the simple act of boiling water and how it changes whatever is placed in it. For example, it softens a hard potato and hardens an egg inside its shell. The temperature of the water is the same, but the result is entirely different. The point was that when we find ourselves in hot water, our reaction will often determine the outcome.

There's no doubt that situations change us. Troubles come our way that we have no control over. Accidents happen. Natural disasters destroy our homes, our possessions, and our animals. We lose our job through no fault of our own. Loved ones leave us either through death or physical distance. Life is filled with tragedies capable of stealing our possessions, our sense of self-worth, our livelihood, and the people we love.

When these things happen, we have two obvious choices. We can view them as part of living and carry on as best we can, or we can check out. If we're surrounded by friends, neighbors, and relatives willing to lend a hand, I think it's easier to claw our way out of sorrow and hard times. As adults, we realize everything is subject to change. If our house insurance or the government covers our losses, we rebuild. Yes, photographs and other treasures are gone, as are those dearest to us, but nothing can take our memories.

However, if we have to face adversities alone, reclaiming self-esteem as well as material objects is more difficult. When people face the same hardships, they tend to pull together, but for a person who has no support system it takes strength of mind and character to go on. That's when we make the decision to harden our outlook on life or accept the challenges and soften our attitude, thus the analogy of the potato and egg.

Sometimes we do both. Often it takes a long time to realize bitterness accomplishes nothing, and it's better to allow hot water to soften us than to make us hard. Even an egg that is transformed from a raw slippery substance is still pliable when cooked in boiling water and then peeled. Perhaps it's best to mourn for a while and then move on no matter how difficult the process might be.

Mom had a protective shell around her I was never able to crack. As much as I loved her, I didn't want such a shell, but as we age we tend to become our mother. If at times I seem hard, I'm still trying to break free of the invisible wall I built as a child to protect myself from the pain life might inflict upon me. It didn't, of course, but I keep chipping at that wall, hoping it will be gone before I join Mom and leave the hot water of life for others to experience.

Turning off the Noise

When I have a hard time falling asleep, I often listen to an audiobook on YouTube. Sometimes it works, but sometimes instead of lulling me to dreamland I start laughing. Such was the case when I chanced upon "The Untethered Soul" by Mike Singer. I listened to the first chapter and knew any chance of sleep was gone. If the following chapters were anything like the first, the humor would keep me awake because it rang true.

Whoever was reading the book should win an award. He read the words as I imagined Singer would have wanted. The first chapter was about the voice in our head that never shuts up. You know what I mean. It's the one that gives us no rest. Even when we're having a good day, the voice tells us there's something to worry about. For example, we're driving down the road, listening to the radio and looking forward to the breakfast we'll soon be enjoying with a friend. Then the voice comes on and says something like, "You know this stretch of road is home to deer," and immediately we start to worry that a deer will run from the bushes and crash into our car. Once we're past that hurdle, the voice doesn't stop tormenting us.

"You're approaching an Amish farm. Better watch out for the horse and buggy." We slow down and peer through the fog, certain that shadowy figure ahead is a horse, a cow, or a child walking alongside the road. Of course, it's only a tree, but the persistent voice refuses to give us even a smidgen of peace. Once we're on Mac Trail, the fear of hitting a deer or a member of the Amish community is over, but the voice doesn't let up. It tells us we probably forgot to turn off the iron or lock the front door.

Even if we're in the safety of our home, the voice is relentless. I can be totally engrossed in an interesting documentary and realize I'm thinking about the columns I haven't written or the grass that needs cutting. I don't want to think about these things. I want to relax and watch the show, but does the voice care? Of course not. It's busy planning its next attack. "Your car windows are down, and it's pouring rain," the voice says. I know perfectly well the windows are up, but then I start to doubt myself. Naturally, I press "pause" and go outside to check. Just as I suspected. The windows are up. All is well.

Bedtime is the most active time for the voice to chant a dozen things guaranteed to steal my sleep. "You forgot to buy flour and eggs when you were in town. Your tires are going flat. You upset your friend when you hung up the phone before she finished talking. The ringing in your ears will probably kill you. You still haven't started writing a chapter for your next book. You need a new hot water heater. That pain jabbing your right side isn't normal. If you keep worrying about everything, all your hair will fall out," and so it goes until I finally get up and take another Xanax.

If I listen to Singer's following chapters, maybe I'll get some pointers on how to silence the voice. It's not my spirit or conscious talking. It's that persistent know-it-all invisible blabbermouth demanding my attention.

You Talk Too Loud

For some unknown reason, I tend to talk with all the power of a gale force wind. I don't know why. I wasn't raised with people who couldn't hear so there was no need to yell my responses as a youngster. However, lately I've noticed my pitch has increased by at least three octaves. Maybe I'm on the verge of going deaf, which is fine with me. I'm looking forward to never again hearing a porcupine gnawing underneath my bedroom window or another mosquito buzzing around my head at 2:00 a.m.

It's like this. When we live alone, we don't realize how annoying we are until someone tells us. We're used to our own company. Our idiosyncrasies might irritate us, but we accept them as the result of years of solitude. Sometimes I burst into song for no reason. Sometimes I sleep on the right side of the bed and sometimes on the left. I have no one to please but myself. If I talk loudly, there's no one to hear and complain.

But every now and then I leave the safety of my metal walls and venture into the world beyond my driveway. That's when I'm made aware the affliction so familiar to me is often a source of annoyance to others. A few days ago, I was shopping at Walmart and asked a salesperson where they hid the molasses. Of course, I couldn't let it go at that. I felt compelled to voice my opinion. I said I wished they would leave things alone and stop rearranging the shelves. The shelf-stocker said she wished I wouldn't talk so loud.

Her words stopped me in my tracks. Egad, I thought. If my dozen words sounded like a thousand horses thundering across the Great Plains, what must I sound like when I utter an entire paragraph? I apologized and said I was losing my hearing and assumed everyone around me was losing theirs. She laughed and said old people were like that. They tended to think the ailments they have are common to everyone and proceeded to give examples. She said there was the lady who forgot her reading glasses and asked "Sally" to assist her with her shopping. The lady went off in a huff when Sally explained she didn't have time because the shelves wouldn't restock themselves.

Sally said she would never forget the elderly gentleman who was dressed as if heading for the racetrack. He wanted to know why the bourbon wasn't down the beer aisle. She told him there was a nice selection of booze towards the front of the store. He said his feet hurt, and it had taken all his energy to walk to the back of the store. He asked Sally to bring him a motorized cart because he didn't think he could walk another half-mile to the front. She countered he must find the energy unless he planned on spending the night in the beer aisle.

It was plain to see that Sally was working herself into what I call an "impotent rage" so I smiled and pushed my cart in what I hoped was the direction of the molasses. After hearing her complaints about other customers, I felt a whole lot better. I might be going deaf but I can still read my list, and I know where to find the bourbon if and when I need it.

Fruit From an Old Tree

There's an old apple tree bordering the ditch in my front yard. I didn't even know it was there until I hired a guy to cut down a dozen spruce trees a few years ago. Due to the lack of space and light, the apple tree grew toward the ditch, so its trunk is more circular than straight. Once I discovered it, I didn't give it much attention. I never noticed any blossoms in the spring, and the fruit it eventually produced was scrawny and fit for nothing but the birds, and even they seemed to avoid it.

Then, as if by a miracle, apples began appearing last summer. Perhaps it was the weather that coaxed them to grow. Perhaps it was the tree's last hurrah. I have no idea, but for the first time since a tiny seed was planted, I harvested a half-bushel of apples. They're free of worms and have not been genetically modified. For consuming out of hand, a dash of salt cuts the tartness. All that's needed for making applesauce is a little sugar and a few spices.

Apple pie with a homemade crust is one of my favorites, so you can be sure a pie is in my oven as I write this. The peelings and cores are in the field behind my home as a treat for any animal that happens upon them. Usually I would have put the trimmings in my compost bin but during the ice storm of January 2020, a poplar crushed the bin and now the job of composting falls to the open field.

When I picked as many apples as I could reach, I knocked down a few more with the aid of a ski pole. While I harvested, I had a little chat with that tree. I thanked it for providing me with an abundant supply of fruit. I praised it for its determination to grow despite the challenges involved in fighting its neighbors for space and light. I extended congratulations on the fine crop it had produced for my benefit as well as the crows, blue jays, and any other bird that had a taste for its fruit. There are still a lot of apples on it, but they're too high for any critter to reach except the birds. The deer are out of luck unless they run through the field where the peelings are.

Sometimes nature gives us gifts we never expected. I didn't think much of that old tree. I didn't have faith in its power to produce. With its crooked spine, it's not a thing of beauty. It looks shabby and unkempt. It's never felt the pinch of pruning shears or heard words of encouragement, yet it never gave up. Instinctively, it knew one day it would succeed and astonish me with its bounty.

It's the same with the weeds we condemn and mow over. Many are edible or useful in making poultices, yet in our ignorance we saturate them with poison and dismiss them as nuisances. Instead of picking berries from our fields, we fill our shopping carts with corporate-grown berries drenched in pesticides. We usually have no idea how to use nature to benefit whatever ails us. The best we can do is admire a sunset, a natural waterfall, a rock formation, or colorful autumn leaves.

I'm glad the apple seed my brother planted as a child rewarded his faith in it. I hope it lives forever, but here's an update. In 2022, the county decided to butcher the tree. Apparently, it hung too far over the ditch and had to go. It wasn't pruned. It was slashed without mercy. Its branches were dismembered and scattered. The apples fell where they were thrown. I cannot bring myself to walk by it, but I hope it knows I did not order its destruction. When others pass by, they will see it as an ugly mess. I'll remember it as a tree that continued to bear fruit even in old age. I wonder how long it will be before I'm considered a nuisance and struck down like my apple tree.

Storage Units Are Everywhere

Is it just me or have you also noticed storage units popping up around our area like mushrooms dotting a cow pasture after a gentle rain? It must be a wonderful feeling to own so much that the bulk of it has to be stored. With winter fast approaching, a storage unit is a must for all the watercrafts that give so much pleasure during the summer months. Everything from a yacht to a jet ski to an old-fashioned rowboat needs a safe place to harbor during the six or seven months of cold weather.

Then there's the snazzy Corvette convertible that must be covered with a custom-made blanket and locked in a secure unit free of rodents that might take a notion to winter in the exhaust pipes. After all, we can hardly blame a mouse or squirrel if it's too stupid to know the difference between a $50,000 Corvette and a $2,000 rattletrap housed in our own garage. If a rodent is dumb enough to stick its head into a well-baited trap, it's certainly incapable of reading a "Keep Out" or "Danger Ahead" sign.

But it's not only the summer vessels and cars that require some TLC during the cold months, it's also the third, fourth, or fifth vehicle we own that needs a home. Factor in the 4-wheelers that belong to each family member, all the mountain bikes, RVs, and a myriad of other things I've never heard of, and a storage unit is an absolute necessity. In these days, there's no free ride. People who used to let their neighbors have gratis garage space are wising up and charging hefty prices. Nobody blames them except the disgruntled freeloaders who can well afford to pay.

I used to watch "Storage Wars" until someone suggested those "miracle" finds were all part of the act and I lost interest. Perhaps there was an occasional find worth great sums of money, but more often than not a unit was filled with items of no value to anyone except the owners. This was especially true if people had no place to live and didn't want to part with their few belongings. They probably paid the first month's rent and didn't have enough cash beyond that. Eventually, their clothes, kitchen items, mattresses, and the kids' toys were auctioned off. If a family is living in a car, there's not much room for luxuries, only hope for a better life.

Now don't get me wrong. I'm not saying people own too much stuff or spend their hard-earned money on non-essentials. They have a right to spend it any way that pleases them. The problem is whatever pleases them one year is often a burden the next and needs to be stored. If they've filled their primary residence, their second home on the lake, their vacation homes in various states, their Florida timeshares, and their hunting cabins, the only option is a storage unit.

My suggestion to anyone who wants to make a buck is to keep building them. I want to see well-maintained storage units on every spare acre of land. I've seen them on M-129, M-28, Six Mile Road, Three Mile Road, and Seymour Road, but I don't get out often so I have no doubt they're springing up throughout the tri-county area.

Storage units are the answer to a shopper's prayer. Don't let them down.

Welcome Autumn

I was walking down the road this morning and noticed the fields were full of vegetation going to seed. I thought about the seasonal cycles and how nature knows when it's time to wrap up one and begin the next. The fields and forests have no calendars or smartphones to alert them to the changes. They just do what they've been doing since the beginning of time. It's something they never tire of, toss aside, or question. Their obedience to the natural flow of things is a reminder that no matter how much man claims dominance over the earth, nature still rules.

While I walked, I heard geese honking as they flew south. Seeing them brought memories of my youth when the sky was dark with hundreds of honkers flying in their V-shaped formation. What a difference time and man have made in the natural flow of things. Now geese no longer fly together by the hundreds. They've learned it's safer to fly in smaller skeins. There's less chance of being shot. There's something wonderfully amazing about geese. When one stays behind due to illness or a wound, another goose will stay by its side until it gets well or dies. Perhaps that's why sometimes we see only one goose as it flies alone in an attempt to catch up with the others. The instinct to remain faithful to the end is a rare quality in human beings, but it is deeply ingrained in the mind of a goose.

The calendar on my desk tells me, autumn has been with us for three weeks. Without much fanfare, it nudged summer aside and was barely noticeable to folks who reside in climates with consistent weather but plainly obvious for those of us in the Upper Peninsula. Soon leaves will drift from the limbs of deciduous trees. Tamaracks will put on their golden display once the leaves of maples, mountain ash, birch, and oak have blanketed the ground. Birdfeeders will be filled with sunflower seeds as chickadees, nuthatches, blue jays, mourning doves, and other birds return for the winter. Squirrels will gather pinecones and acorns and stack them in various places around the yard or in the garage. Bears will seek out the last of the berries and find a place to spend the winter. Rodents will burrow underneath deserted buildings.

October is a reflective time for me. Many years ago the previous month robbed my daughter of her grandfather, my Dad. Stephanie missed rides on the tractor, helping him with minor chores, and putting the last piece of a jigsaw puzzle in place. He was given such a short time to love her and given no time at all to tell her about life on the farm. He wasn't here for her first birthday, having passed away six weeks prior to it. Dad slipped from us as silently as one season gives way to the next.

And so it goes. Changes occur, sometimes welcome, sometimes dreaded, and the cycle of life—whether nature's or human— continues. We marvel as autumn leaves turn our world into a kaleidoscope of red, orange, rust, and yellow. The colors beckon us from the comfort of our homes and the trappings of modern technology. For a brief moment, we drive down roads where canopies of sugar maples meet overhead. We're reminded of our school days when we searched the woods for the biggest and best leaves to gather, bring home, and wax for an assignment.

As I write this the late afternoon sun is filling my room with an orange glow as it filters through my drapes. The faux lace curtains leave patterns on my desk and the floor. I follow the shadow created by the branches of spruce trees as they move across my room. The day is slowly coming to an end as the sun sinks lower in the sky, making room for dusk and the passing of another day, another autumn.

The Upside-Down Chicken

Throughout my lifetime I've probably roasted less than three turkeys. I was twenty-one and a new bride when I attempted my first bird. I was proud of it until my husband asked what I had done with the giblets. I said the turkey didn't have any. When Chuck reached into the bird and pulled them out of the neck or the rear end—I don't remember which—he realized I hadn't given our dinner a proper bath. Despite that oversight, we dined royally and survived our first Thanksgiving without an attack of botulism.

I don't recall the other turkeys I roasted, but I do recollect the one and only chicken that landed in my oven. It was forty years later and I wanted to impress a friend who didn't much care for my vegetarian dishes. In anticipation of the occasion, I purchased a roaster from my pals at QVC. Then I asked a butcher for advice on which bird to buy. When the appointed day arrived, I gave Chicken a thorough cleaning inside and out, rubbed her with butter and seasoned her well with sea salt, cracked pepper and sage before placing her in the roaster.

While she cooked I made all the sides and admitted the delicious aroma spreading throughout my kitchen and spilling into the living room was enticing. Maybe eating poultry was a good idea, I said to myself, and wondered why I had been shunning the flesh of beef, pork, and birds for so long. When Guest arrived and Chicken was ready, I was proud of my achievement. Guest complimented my cooking ability and said it was the moistest chicken he had ever consumed.

Naturally, I thanked him and said the praise belonged to the butcher who was responsible for picking out the best bird. Guest said he didn't think it was the butcher who deserved all the credit. He said it was my brilliant idea of roasting the chicken upside down. He said he'd never seen that done before, but it was a technique he would remember and pass along to his other lady friends. He said some of their chickens were so dry he choked on their breasts and had to settle for their thighs.

I assured him roasting a bird upside down was a trick my dear departed mother had taught me. I explained she said allowing the juices to run down the front instead of the back made all the difference. He nodded and swallowed the lie as quickly as he swallowed the meal and went on his way. After he left, I knew I would never again roast anything that had two legs. If I couldn't tell the difference between the breast and the backside, I had no business pretending I did.

A Gift in the Woods

There's a retired fellow I know who built a structure in the woods. It started out as a simple shack where men could gather in November, shoot deer, and swap stories around the campfire. It was what you might call an outdoor man cave.

When year after year the guys complained about the cold, and few deer appeared, the fellow decided to enlarge the shack. He downed trees, put up walls, nailed on a metal roof, cut holes for windows, made shutters, and hung a door. These projects took two summers of steady labor. In the fall, he installed a small Franklin stove and built a loft. The shack had become a rustic cabin. He made hooks for hunting clothes and shelves for miscellaneous gear. He built a front porch, an outdoor bench, and a lean-to for wood. He felled more trees and filled the storage area with a supply of birch.

At some point, he made a table and bought old chairs he found at a yard sale. He searched his outdoor sheds for kerosene lanterns, rifle racks, and cast iron frying pans. He found picturesque outdoor scenes which he hung on the cabin walls. Eventually he built an outhouse. In the evening, with his dog by his side, he watched the sun set from the cabin's porch and enjoyed the solitude and beauty of his surroundings.

The third spring, he started work on an addition. Another summer passed before the room was finished. The simple deer blind had become a lodge. By now he had grandchildren. They were too young to appreciate the wonderful gift their grandpa had built for them, but every now and then their parents brought them out and they roasted hot dogs and marshmallows around the campfire.

I was talking to this fellow the other day. He said it's been many years since anyone spent a night at the lodge, and nobody uses it as a hunting camp. Maybe it's too rustic or too outdated. He said his days of improving it are gone. He doesn't have the physical stamina or the desire to continue building something nobody shows an interest in. I don't think he's completely given up, but folks tend to lose heart when something meaningful to them doesn't mean much to others.

Maybe someday someone will discover the magical place he created. I hope so because it's a shame the work of my brother's hands stands forlorn and forgotten. But maybe life is like that. We build things we think are special and important. Things that tell people who we are, but maybe our gifts of labor and love are meant only for our eyes—something we can look at and remember as we grow old.

A Well-Stacked Woodpile

When October winds blow over September's fallen leaves, woodsheds should be well-stocked and stacked to the rafters. If this winter is anything like the last one, woodstoves, furnaces, and fireplaces will get a daily workout trying to keep the house warm. Although I don't heat with wood, one of my favorite chores is helping my brother ready his supply for the winter.

We have a system. Ed cuts, blocks, and splits the wood. Each year I stack it outside and the following summer I bring it in. I get out my favorite wheelbarrow, load it up, wheel it to his shed, and stack it where it's close by and ready for cold weather. There was a time when I never gave a second thought to the winter's wood supply. In the old days, Dad used a buzzsaw powered by his tractor. There was no such thing as a fancy wood splitter to do the job. The closest I came to helping was walking by the workers and holding my ears because I couldn't stand the noise. Occasionally, I brought glasses of cold water or cans of Black Label to Dad and whoever was helping him buzz the wood that was headed for our kitchen stove.

My attitude changed a number of years ago, and I realized I enjoyed the challenge of working with wood. It was early November and my gift of labor was my birthday present to my brother. I bartered the use of a splitter, wrestled the logs Ed had already blocked, and ran the splitter's blade through each piece as easily as a warm knife slices through cold butter. Then I wheeled the wood to his shed. I had no idea how to begin stacking, but I wanted to surprise Ed when he came home from work so I did the best I could. I don't know if he was more surprised at his full woodshed or at my stacking style. As a novice, I had criss-crossed every stick, unaware such an endeavor was a waste of space and time. Each year I've gotten better at my favorite chore, but one thing remains constant. I never know what will pop out of the woodpile. This summer yielded two brown garter snakes, a green one, crickets, slugs, ants, spiders, and one blue spotted salamander. I interrupted his nap when I overturned a fallen log where he had been resting. The ticks weren't a problem. I guess they'd had their fill of me earlier in the summer.

As the days get cooler, wood smoke will scent the air on calm autumn mornings as neighbors fire up their wood-burning furnaces and my brother gets a fire going in his stove. His kitchen will be warmed by the Heartland cook stove reminiscent of the one in our old kitchen. His is much fancier than the Hotpoint Mom cooked on, but it brings back memories. Our stove burned every day regardless of the weather. In winter, it threw off enough heat to take the chill off the kitchen, but in summer we roasted along with our dinner.

As we gallop into the 21st century, there seems to be a trend towards all things country. Magazines abound with stories and pictures from the past, lending a romantic nostalgia to a bygone era. Those of us who lived in that era must sometimes wonder how we missed all the beauty of the old days. When I turn the pages of modern magazines, I see lovely rooms decorated with lots of familiar antiques, but I've yet to see a functioning water pump in the kitchen, an upstairs commode, or the necessary outdoor privy.

People collect items to display on shelves made from barn wood, but I don't recall any such shelves in our house or displays of butter churns, wash tubs, or kerosene lamps. Such things weren't meant for display. They were necessities. Long before I was born, if Gram wanted butter, she reached for the jars of cream in the ice box, got out the butter churn, and went to work. Prior to getting a wringer washing machine, Mom scrubbed our clothes on a washboard she plunged into a granite tub. Kerosene lamps were called into use before the REA ran a power line down our road. Telephones were unheard of.

When I was a kid, there wasn't one iota of romance involved in awaking to a freezing cold house. Like most country homes, ours was not insulated. There was nothing to stop the cold from penetrating the walls and taking up residence in our rooms. We could scratch our names on the frost on the windows. Linoleum floors were cold as ice. The trip to the outhouse sent shivers throughout our limbs and everywhere else. There was no point in complaining. Living like a homesteading pioneer was taken for granted. Whether we liked it or not, that's just the way it was.

Well anyway, my brother's wood is in and we're none the worse for wear. We have a few remaining outside chores to complete before the snow falls, but what doesn't get done will have to wait until spring. To while away the winter hours, I'm thinking of subscribing to various country magazines. As I look through the pages, I'll laugh at the pristine homes bearing no resemblance to the house of my childhood.

Requiem for My Steel Toe Boots

For years, my steel toe boots served me well when called into use. Every summer and fall, I pulled them out of the closet and headed for the woods. As my brother felled and blocked birch trees, it was my job to throw the wood into the open field. Once there, it was placed in a cart behind the tractor and hauled to his front yard. He handled the log splitter while I did the stacking. More than once my boots cushioned the blow of a piece of birch as it slipped from my hands and dropped on my toes.

But everything comes to an end, and eventually our days of cutting and stacking were over. My brother moved downstate and weeds have overtaken his log splitter. A couple days ago I was looking for a hammer in my closet and came across my boots. They were right where I had left them two years earlier after stacking my last piece of hardwood. I took them out and as I wiped away the dust, I noticed what looked like a row of teeth across the toe. At first I thought a rodent had nibbled on each one, but then I realized the strange sight was the result of many years of toil. The leather had simply worn out.

A wave of nostalgia rushed over me as I held those boots. My Georgia Giant, oil resistant, steel toes held memories of happier days when I was agile and looked forward to working with the wood. Every morning when I laced them on, I knew I was ready for hours of outdoor labor. They never let me down. They were as steadfast as a faithful friend. Anyone who owns a pair knows what I mean.

My first thought was to give them to a resale shop. The boots have years of service left in them. The interior's like new and with a quick rub of neatsfoot or mink oil, the exterior will look the same. I have high arches and the inserts I wore with them were tucked into the boots. They showed wear and without a word told the story of their days working with the wood better than I could. I took them out and threw them in the trash.

Like so many things I've discarded or lost over the years, I had forgotten about my boots. It irritates me that an inanimate object can stir so many memories of hours spent working with a loved one. My brother and I never quarreled. Those years of handling wood brought us closer together than we had ever been. I have a feeling I'm not quite ready for the requiem.

Get Ready for Christmas Craft Shows

Brimley welcomes the holidays with a Christmas craft show on the first Saturday in November. This is a major event for folks who love to purchase homemade items for themselves or give as gifts. Everyone looks forward to seeing what goodies are available. I'm always intrigued by the variety of items. I enjoy looking at the homemade wreaths, mittens, hats, jewelry, and food, but my favorite stop is at the vendors who sell kitchen cutting boards. Last year I bought three in different shapes and sizes. I admire folks who are talented and can turn pieces of wood into art. The strips of maple and birch vary in color and design and are absolutely beautiful.

Naturally, the boards are much too pretty to use. Whenever I need to cut anything, I reach for the board I purchased years ago from Walmart. I can't bring myself to cut an onion, potato, or even a stalk of celery on a fancy board. When I have coffee in the morning, I sit at my place and admire my collection. That's another benefit to living alone. I don't have to explain why I buy something meant to be functional when I know perfectly well its only function in my kitchen will be ornamental.

Collectors share a common bond. We appreciate the aesthetic beauty of handmade art whether it's in the form of a painting, a glass bulb for the Christmas tree, or a cutting board. We need an occasional break from the mundane. If we can't afford a Monet original or a copy of Rodin's "The Thinker," we can shell out a few dollars for an item that appeals to our sense of beauty. Throughout November and half of December, I'll be attending craft shows because I know I'll find something too cute not to bring home. Anyone who makes the yearly jaunt to various high school gyms or town halls knows there's always a surprise waiting for them.

And it's not just the purchasing that makes the shows interesting. It's talking to the folks who spend months making the items they sell. Everyone has a story. Some ladies knit or crochet to pass the time and didn't think about selling their stuff until someone suggested they do. Budding entrepreneurs have workshops where they create duck decoys, bird houses, or furniture made from barn wood. Seamstresses sit at their sewing machines constructing fancy dresses for little girls and their dolls. Soap makers experiment with various shades and fragrances, and makers of candles do likewise. The list of unique items available for sale is endless.

Christmas shopping at malls, Walmart, or even online can be a nightmare. Everyone's rushing to find the perfect gift. Whether they're shopping on Black Friday or Cyber Monday, the hunt is on and it's not pretty. Contrast the mad scene at brick-and-mortar or internet stores with the pleasant atmosphere of craft shows and it's easy to see why many folks prefer the latter. Everyone is friendly and knowledgeable about what they're selling. They're willing to spend time with customers and answer questions. The creations might be a little pricier than something from China, but they're worth it. Consider the time involved in making a piece of original art. Whether it's a beautiful cedar wreath for your front door or a lamp made from an empty bottle of Bailey's Irish Crème, homemade items are well worth the cost.

Wouldn't it be amazing if people turned back the clock and had an old-fashioned Christmas, one void of electronic gadgets, smartphones, and computerized toys? Imagine the look of shock on a youngster's face as he unwrapped a book instead of the drone he was expecting. Or the girl who received paper dolls instead of another Barbie. Or the wife who opened a box of Queen Anne Chocolate Covered Cherries instead of an "Ask Google Home Wireless Assistant." Or the husband who got a box of hankies in place of the assault weapon he had requested. If only for one Christmas, pocketbooks would still have money left in them come December 26. But, of course, family members would be furious and probably wouldn't speak to each other until their "real" gifts were distributed by parents beaten into submission by their children or each other.

Waterbed Woes

Over the years, I've had the opportunity to meet some interesting characters. In the 1970s, one such fellow was a graduate student earning his PhD in economics from Wayne State University (WSU) in Detroit. Funds were scarce and his living conditions were not the best. He rented an old mobile home in an impoverished neighborhood. He said it wasn't a bad place to live until cold weather hit, and he didn't have enough money to pay his fuel bill. As the temperature dropped, so, too, did his spirits.

His one extravagance had been the purchase of a waterbed. He was immensely proud of that bed. He said it was ideal for him because he had insomnia. The soothing sound of water sloshing whenever he moved helped lull him back to sleep. He said he forgot all about his money troubles as he dreamed about the future when his financial state would be greatly improved. He was studying to be a

CPA and upon graduation had dreams of earning more money than he could ever spend.

When winter was in full swing, he said a good night's rest became more challenging. As the outside temperature fell, it also fell inside. His once comfortable bed began to adjust to the elements. One morning when he awakened, his bedroom was colder than usual, and when he rolled out of bed he said the water didn't slosh. He quickly dressed and headed for campus. In his haste to reach the warmth of Old Main, he neglected to securely close his front door. Old Man Winter saw his chance, entered the trailer, and went straight for the bedroom.

Instead of going home after classes, the fellow decided to spend a few hours researching Descartes, Locke, Hume, and Smith at the Detroit Public Library. That library is housed in a beautiful building. I, too, spent many hours there when I attended WSU. My friend said he was deep in thought reading fascinating articles pertaining to the economic philosophy of the masters. He stayed at the library until closing time. When he finally left, he was surprised to see that a great amount of snow had fallen. He hurried home.

The cold he felt when entering his humble abode was nothing compared to the shock awaiting him in the bedroom. As he whiled away the afternoon studying economics, he never gave a thought to thermodynamics. It was only when he rolled onto his bed he realized the water had frozen. He was left with a block of ice. He said his fondness for waterbeds quickly evaporated. He quickly found new digs in Cass Corridor, where crime was less a concern for him than a frozen waterbed.

Part V:
Our Family Life
in the 1950s

Stay In Or Stay Out

When I was a kid the sound of the kitchen screen door slamming irritated Mom to no end. As youngsters, my siblings and I couldn't figure out why she made such a fuss over something so trivial. In the old days screen doors slammed. That's just the way it was unless we took time to gently close the door. Nobody was going to do that when summer had finally arrived and warm sunshine beckoned us outside.

"Stay in or stay out," was Mom's favorite mantra. In those days we had no more idea what a mantra was than we knew how the radio worked. We only knew we heard that saying from sunup to sundown. If we had been creative, we could have amused ourselves by writing jingles that rhymed with Mom's words. But we weren't creative and we weren't very obedient either, because I don't think we ever stopped slamming that door. We didn't do it on purpose. We just never thought to slow down as we ran out of the kitchen. It's taken me seven decades to understand why such a noise bothered Mom, but I finally agree with her. The spring in my door doesn't work anymore. Now I hear myself repeating Mom's words whenever I hear the slap of my screen door.

Why does it take us so long to appreciate the things our mother said and did? Saving a tea bag after one use didn't make sense to me when I was young. Why save one when there were plenty more in the Lipton box? Guess who saves teabags now? Yup, you're right, but unlike Mom I only save the bag for one day. Draw an extra pail of water in case the lights go out during a storm was another ritual we considered silly. Now I get it, but instead of going to the wellhouse for water, I merely turn the tub faucet and fill a plastic pail instead of a granite one.

I bet I could fill this page with all the things Mom did and said. I don't know who declared that as we grow older our mother grows wiser, but they were right. Given enough time, "they" are usually right about everything. A stitch in time does save nine. Counting our chickens before they hatch will guarantee the eggs were never fertilized. If we don't look before we leap, we're sure to land in a pile of manure.

If we started quoting Poor Richard's Almanac to the grandkids they'd drop us off at the nearest Old Folks Home. Luckily for me, I have no grandchildren. I'm going to keep repeating Mom's sayings until my stay here is over.

Dressing for Cold Weather

When my sister and I were kids and went outside to play or do chores, Mom made sure our every-day overalls were patched, the buttons on our jackets were securely sewn in place, and bandanas protected our hair and ears. Often Jude didn't bother wearing headgear. She told Mom her hair was thick enough to protect her ears from the wind, and she didn't care if her hair was blown every which way because her curls were natural and naturally went in whatever direction they chose. Sometimes she didn't even bother to button her jacket. I was just the opposite. I buttoned and zipped my outerwear up to my neck, wrapped a woolen scarf tightly around my neck, and always wore something on my head. When we wore our work clothes, we would not have won a "best dressed" contest. Today's kids would be horrified if their mother made them wear anything close to our getups, but we didn't know any different.

For you see, in the old days that's how things were. Good clothes were never worn anywhere except to school, church, or the occasional Friday night trip to Sault Ste. Marie. When we played outside, we thought nothing of wearing apparel that was patched or stained. If our overalls were too long, we simply rolled them up. If jackets were too small and our arms were exposed to the autumn weather, we endured the cool air without complaint. After all, arms couldn't catch cold or get an earache so it was no big deal. The whole idea of being outside was to have fun whether that meant playing in the haymow, checking an empty manger in the barn for a new litter of kittens, or getting out a bat and ball for a quick game if Mom's friends had brought their children to play with us. I don't remember what the game was called, but the batter only had to run to first base and back. There were two batters, one pitcher, a couple fielders, and a kid who acted as first baseman.

As Mom visited with her lady friends, we found ways to amuse ourselves. Staying in the house was unthinkable especially if it was a sunny day. The only time we stopped playing was when we were called in for lunch. We ran back outside as soon as the last spoonful of chili was consumed and our glass of milk was empty. One memory of my Dafter cousins that stuck with me throughout all the years was their absolute reluctance to drink that lousy "cow's milk" Mom kept in a quart jar in the fridge. Although my male cousins had other relatives who lived on farms, somehow the boys couldn't make the connection between milk in a Mason jar and milk in one of Osborn Dairy's glass jugs. My memory doesn't reach back far enough to recall whether they did drink the milk once Mom mixed a helping of Nestles Quick in the glass to camouflage the white stuff that came straight from Daisy's udder or if they refused all milk—regardless of the color—in favor of a glass of water. Well water at that.

Ah, the good old days when kids played outside in all kinds of weather, dressed in clothes that today would be considered rags, and drank unpasteurized milk or water that came from the ground instead of a bottle labeled "purified." Those days are gone forever, but I remember a time when life on the farm was all we knew. I can't help but think we're all the better for it.

A First Communion Story

One Sunday morning in the summer of 1954, I was all gussied up in my First Communion clothes. My dress and veil and lacy white socks were beautiful, but I looked the same as every other Sunday—ugly. My dress had short sleeves, and there was a big scab on my right arm. I had fallen on the gravel when I was on my bicycle and had run over a dead toad. Mom said the scab was God's punishment because I should have buried the toad, not driven it further into the road. I said the toad was already half-buried and I was just finishing the job.

I reached for my new white shoes and took them out of the box. The man at the shoe store said he'd never seen such long, skinny feet. He made me feel like a freak. I thought salesmen had more sense than to insult a kid when their Mom was putting out good money to buy new shoes, but what did I know?

The nuns had told us we had to wear white everywhere because now we would be little brides of Christ. That was the last thing I wanted to be. I wanted to be the bride of Jerome Bitters but he wasn't Catholic so even at the tender age of seven, I knew that would never happen. I had to settle for sitting beside him in class and dreaming about him before falling asleep. Sister Mary Margaret had told us we'd probably die horrible deaths if we didn't marry Catholics. I thought God didn't even like us or He wouldn't have made all the Catholic boys so homely.

When we finally got to church, I was scared. I was the tallest kid and was supposed to bring up the rear. Mom had warned me not to trip and fall because she said coming in last was the most important spot, and everybody would be watching. I told her I wouldn't fall, but my stomach was churning like a butter paddle. She said I'd be fine and told me not to walk too fast down the aisle and not to chew the host. She said I had to keep my eyes on the floor when I walked back to my pew and not look around like a crow on a fence post.

I have no idea how I survived that Sunday, but I did. I didn't fall or chew the host or embarrass Mom, but I sure was glad when mass was over. Dad stopped at Horsefeather's and bought us ice cream cones. Mine was chocolate. Only one drip fell on my lovely new First Communion dress that was hung on a hanger and forgotten.

The Lawnmower Episode

When I was young, the thought of owning a lawnmower was as foreign to us as fresh strawberries in February. There was no need for a mower because we had milk cows. Once a week a few trustworthy bossies were allowed to eat the grass in our front yard. Our cattle were as tame as housecats. I don't remember who watched them, but I know it wasn't me. Most likely Jude stood guard and waved a little switch if they meandered too close to the road.

One summer Mom decided it was time to cut the grass like normal people. Jude walked across the road and borrowed Uncle Steve's lawnmower, the very thought of which sent shivers down her spine. At fifteen, my sister was fearless of anything with four legs, but a lawnmower was a different matter. Once the machine was ready for action, I sat on the porch and watched her walk the length of our yard with all the gusto of a kid starting kindergarten.

Her greatest fear wasn't the amount of grass that needed cutting or the length and width of the yard or the amount of time and energy required for the job. Her greatest fear was hitting stones or dog bones hidden in the tall timothy. In the old days, our dogs chewed on beef bones then buried them, but sometimes not very deep. You know what Job said about his greatest fear coming true? Well, what was true in Biblical times was also true in 1958. As Jude gained confidence in her task, she became less diligent in keeping an eye out for obstacles in her path. Her gait increased, her attention wandered, and she failed to see the bone until she hit it.

When the machine stopped and Jude went down, I was sure she was dead. According to an entry in my old diary, it was July 9, a day that lived forever in the mind of my sister. Little pieces of bone went through her overalls and grazed her leg, but the pain of that was insignificant compared to the fear lawnmowers instilled in her for the rest of her life. Mom had a fit that her brother's mower was ruined, but Dad took things in stride. After looking it over, he said it just needed a new blade. Everybody calmed down and Jude limped to the house. She said the cows did a better job than the machine, and she vowed never to go near it again. No amount of coaxing got her close to our own lawnmower when my parents finally bought one years later.

Should Jude have kept a sharp eye out for stones and dog bones? Should Waggs have buried it deeper? Absolutely.

Sipping Through a Straw

Summer is the perfect time to get out the straws and sip your favorite drink. When I was a youngster, there was always a box of paper straws in the kitchen cupboard and a pitcher of cold lemonade or Kool-Aid in the refrigerator. Jude was the self-appointed lemonade maker. I'm sure it didn't occur to her to wash the lemons prior to cutting and squeezing them by hand on the glass lemon juicer that was in every kitchen across America. I'm also sure I complained when she dumped the seeds into the pitcher along with the juice. Jude was not fussy.

On warm summer days, we filled our glasses and stuck straws in them. We didn't have ice cubes because our freezer compartment was smaller than a breadbox. There wasn't enough room for ice cube trays, but we didn't care. We had great fun blowing bubbles until they threatened to overflow our glass. That would have resulted in a sticky mess that would have attracted flies, so bubble blowing was strictly an outdoor activity. Once we left the kitchen, we blew with all the strength of a northwest wind. At least that's how I remember things, but memories have the potential of leaning a little to the left or right of the truth.

Along with blowing bubbles, Mom could not abide us sipping until we reached the bottom of the glass, at which time quiet sipping turned into a hideous slurping noise. When the straw connected with the last few drops of whatever was in the glass, there was nothing remotely ladylike about that sound. Mom said slurping was obnoxious. It wasn't nice. It was a display of bad manners. It was rude. She was always concerned about how our behavior looked to others. She tried to instill in us the importance of being earnest, if you'll pardon the pun. Table etiquette was a top priority.

We lived in a house lacking modern plumbing and heating. Mom cooked our meals on a woodstove. We had barn manure on our boots. Our bathroom was an outhouse. Mom said none of these things mattered because they were irrelevant to being a lady. Good manners reached beyond the house, and good manners dictated that a lady did not slurp.

Today my straw reached the bottom of my strawberry shake. Guess what I did. Yes, I slurped, not to dishonor Mom's memory, but to get every last drop of my $4 strawberry milkshake from Burger King.

The Power of Heet

The other day I decided it was time to see what was lurking in the dark corners of the cabinet underneath my bathroom sink. Nothing had been disturbed since 1971 so I figured whatever was there was probably out of date. Some things like band-aids in a metal tin and Vicks Vapor Rub never expire, but glass bottles of Pepto Bismol or Listerine are entirely different matters.

To my surprise the most memorable things I discovered were Johnson & Johnson Adhesive Tape in a metal container, a bottle of Watkins Liniment so old it was cloudy instead of clear, and an unopened bottle of Heet. For readers too young or too healthy to remember, I'll explain. Heet was the name of an analgesic liniment made in the U.S.A. by Whitehall Laboratories. It was sold in a dark brown bottle with a red label surrounded by flames. Attached to the cap was an applicator dabber much like those found in a bottle of shoe polish. With one twist of the cap, a person could easily cure their aches and pains by rolling the brush over the affected areas. Heet was one of these strange things that fascinated me as a child.

On the back of the bottle was a cautionary note, but when I was eight my reading ability was limited to the adventures of Dick, Jane, and their dog, Spot. I should have ignored the liniment as soon as I saw the flames, but you know how kids are. I had watched Dad and Gram roll the stuff on their knees and although I didn't like the smell, I liked the orange color. One day when Dad was at work, Gram was asleep on her cot and nobody else was in the kitchen, I took the bottle from the medicine cabinet. I sat on the daybed in the front room and unscrewed the top, which was no easy task. Arrows pointed in the direction I was supposed to turn, but I struggled to get the bottle open.

When at last I succeeded, I had great fun rolling the dabber up one leg and down the other. My legs didn't ache but they were covered with hair. I hated that hair and thought the liniment would melt it off. When I finished doctoring, I put the bottle back and waited. It didn't take long for Heet to do its job. My legs were on fire. I ran to the kitchen, lifted one of the water pails from the table and stepped in it. My experiment of ridding hair from my legs was a total and complete failure. The hair remained in place until I was a teenager and allowed to rub it off with a sandpaper mitt.

I don't remember what Mom said when she got home and saw me standing in our drinking water, but I know I never touched Heet again. Sometimes it takes kids years to realize when a parent tells them not to touch something, it's for their own good. Some of us had to learn that lesson the hard way.

A Memory of Old Spice

Every woman past sixty will remember giving her father a bottle of Old Spice aftershave as a present. At least, that's my memory. I wish I could recall the fragrance, but I can't. I just remember seeing that white opaque bottle in the medicine cabinet. Dad had to be coaxed into splashing some on every Sunday morning when we went to church. Any other day of the week was out of the question. The cows didn't care how good he smelled as long as he was at the barn twice a day for their milking.

In times of old, choices were limited in the men's aftershave department. Fellows weren't as vain as they are now. They didn't need pampering. They were satisfied with a slap of Old Spice on their face and a brush cut from the nearest barbershop. They wouldn't have set foot in a beauty parlor intended for women. They didn't worry about which hairstyle suited them best or if they should experiment with dyes and perms.

Dad would laugh if he were still with us. He and his buddies wouldn't believe how much things have changed. They'd remember the days when a man was judged by his character, not his haircut or aroma. As men are continuing to be pushed into connecting with their "feminine" side, their masculinity often takes a beating. Old-timers will remember when a man's hands were strong and calloused, and their fingernails had never met a manicurist. Some fellows were embarrassed about their rough hands and apologized, but there was no need. Like our face, our hands tell the story of our life much more than any fragrance or hair style could.

Dad's ring finger on his left hand was always stiff. When I asked what happened, he laughed and said he was attempting to steal a pie cooling on a windowsill when the lady of the house saw him and her knife connected with his finger. For years I believed that story. Mom eventually told me the truth. Dad's finger had been caught in a piece of farm machinery. When I visited him shortly before his passing, I held his hand and learned the meaning of "in the midst of death, there is life." The finger that had been stiff for most of his life was as flexible as mine. I held his hand for a long time.

Whenever I see Old Spice on a store shelf, I think of Sunday mornings, Dad, and that opaque bottle. I hope fathers still receive gifts that bring pleasant memories to their daughters long after their dad has passed.

Picking the Scab

We all do it. It's part of human nature. It's something we can't resist no matter how hard we try. We might as well admit it. We're a nation of scab pickers. As soon as a wound heals over, we can't wait to pick off the scab and watch a new one form. I don't know why we're programmed to make such a move. We know it's wrong. We know it inhibits the healing process, but we can't stop ourselves.

Scab picking is a hobby for most children—at least it was in the old days. Our knees were constantly victims of our play. We ran, we fell, we bled, we bandaged, and we waited. We knew it would take a few days for a scab to form so we usually didn't peek underneath the bandage. In those days, they had a lot of stick to them. Prying one loose was almost as painful as the injury we sustained from the fall.

Elbows often got skinned when we lost control of our bicycle and landed on the gravel. Sharp stones took their toll. No body part was safe from a fall on the road, especially if we were pedaling at breakneck speed. I was a coward so I never pedaled fast, but the boys who lived down the road were daredevils. It wasn't unusual to see them flying down one hill and up the other.

Although I have no proof, I suppose they were masters at picking scabs. Their arms and legs must have been covered with them. Boys are notorious for picking things. When it was haying time and wire from a square bale scratched the length of their arms, I imagine they couldn't wait for scabs to form. Scratches like that meant plenty of good picking.

I wonder if this tendency is a carryover from our days as primates. Apes still groom each other. Maybe that's what we were doing. We'd look silly pulling the scab off someone else's body so we stick to picking our own. A credible theory perhaps, but one certainly open to debate.

When Patches Were Popular

Mom patched the knees of our overalls with bits of fabric cut from items found in the rag bag. Every mother had a bag full of scraps of material destined to be recycled. We had never heard the term "recycle" because it wasn't in vogue in the 1950s. However, when our knees started showing, we knew it was time to dig through the rag bag and find an appropriate piece of fabric for our mother to sew over the holes.

Patching began when the day's work was done, and we were tucked in our beds. Mom listened to the radio as she mended the holes by stitching the patches in place. Sometimes one patch covered another one on clothes that were never worn to school or any other public place. People would have thought us destitute, felt sorry for us, and perhaps passed the hat if they saw us attending a function in patched clothing. We would have been embarrassed and humiliated. We had no way of knowing that decades later holes in jeans would be all the rage and considered "fashionable."

Why are people so gullible? Why do we find it necessary to fall in line with the herd and go along with something our common sense tells us is stupid? Have we lost the ability to think for ourselves and form our own opinions? Are we afraid to buck the crowd? Anyone with the slightest pinch of common sense knows wearing clothes full of holes is comical if not downright absurd. It's also incredibly expensive. Wealthy people can afford to look ridiculous in ripped, skintight jeans, but we would laugh ourselves silly if a friend or relative showed up looking like a clown.

How long will the holey jean rage continue? Fads usually fizzle out after a year or two when people come to their senses and realize they've been made fools of by clever marketing schemes. If Bill Gates or Warren Buffett started a "Go Fund Me" page, would anyone be idiotic enough to make a contribution? Probably not, so why do people contribute to designers who create and stores that sell ripped, shredded, slashed, frayed, faded, and dirty-looking jeans?

I'm baffled by a lot of things and second on the list is purchasing clothing fit only for the rag bag. I asked Google to tell me some of the stores that sell these outrageously expensive tattered and torn rags. Abercrombie & Fitch came in at the low end with a price tag of $99. These jeans would be considered cheap because the only slashes they have are across the knees. No true fashionista would ever stoop to wearing such poorly made clothing.

Saks was offering women's "ripped logo lined" Balenciaga jeans for $995. I suppose the black lining bumped up the price, but one look at the final product would scare you. The sad news is not only women have been duped. Intelligent men also jumped on the "I'm crazy about rags" wagon. In 2017, Nordstrom bought a line of men's muddy-looking jeans and matching jackets costing $425-$595 that are still in style. Fellows with deep pockets will take home Givenchy's "straight distressed jeans" for a mere $1995. Unfortunately, they don't carry sizes larger than 38 so heftier gents are out of luck.

Mom spent hours patching and washing our overalls. Little did she know that years later it would be considered the height of fashion to wear raggedy, mud-stained clothing. Had she known all she had to do was cut more holes in the knees and swish our jeans and jackets in mud puddles, she could have saved herself time and energy and perhaps gone to bed a little earlier than midnight. But who would have guessed that the 21st century jean fad would be rags full of holes?

Let's Churn Some Butter

I was visiting a friend last week and spied an old-fashioned butter churn shoved in a corner of Edwina's living room. Upon closer inspection, I realized it was a duplicate of the one I remembered from my childhood. Like ours, my friend's was about a foot high and made of glass. A wooden paddle was attached to the metal lid and a red wooden handle was used to churn the cream into butter.

Just looking at that churn brought back memories of the day my sister and I decided to try our hand at making butter. Our old churn had been pushed aside and forgotten in the spare room above the kitchen. Jude had an idea. She told me to go upstairs and get the churn. There was a jar of milk in the refrigerator. On top of the milk was a thick layer of cream. Nobody was home and our chores were done. We were going to surprise our parents with a gift of homemade butter.

Jude skimmed the cream from the milk and put it in the churn. We had no idea how much cream it took to make a block of butter, but the amount we put in didn't look like much because the paddle couldn't reach it. Jude added milk. Once the lid was securely in place, she put all her strength into turning the paddle. I was fascinated at the speed my sister achieved. Within seconds, the sides of the jar were covered with cream. I was sure the churn would break and the broken glass and milky substance would be splattered all over the place. Eventually she slowed her pace and kept going.

I asked when it was my turn. She said to be patient which meant she had no intention of relinquishing the handle. That is, not until the phone rang and I refused to answer it. She put that heavy churn underneath one arm and kept turning the handle with the other as she went to the front room where the phone was.

Her conversation lasted only a minute. Like a shot, she was back in the kitchen, put the churn on the table and said it was all mine. She was going bike riding with a friend who lived down the road. It was up to me to finish the job. I was thrilled but had no idea how long the process would take. I churned that cream until I thought my arm would fall off and still I couldn't make butter. Finally, I gave up and dumped the goopy mess into the slop pail, washed the churn, and put it back where it belonged. When Jude got home she asked where the butter was. I pointed to the pail and said there wasn't any butter only milky globs that were good for nothing but the pigs.

Edwina's churn stirred up memories of the day I realized how nice it was to have store-bought butter.

Independence Day and the Seed Spitting Contest

The Fourth of July is traditionally a day of celebration with parades, picnics, fireworks, and friends getting together to celebrate our independence. When I was a kid, I didn't give a hoot about the British or the Revolutionary War. I was much more interested in the sparklers than any old Redcoat. I couldn't wait until I was handed a little gray stick that came to life after dark. Once the end was lit, we had great fun waving the sparklers. It was one of those magical childhood moments.

Although we lived ten miles from Sault Ste. Marie, sometimes we could see the fireworks lighting the sky if we stood on the back porch. We never went to town and joined the crowd. My siblings and I didn't think we were missing much. We were satisfied with our sparklers and absolutely delighted if allowed to hold one in each hand.

July 4th meant much more than bright sparks shooting into the cool night air. It also signaled the first watermelon of the season. In those days, watermelons weren't available every month of the year. Summer was the only time they were in the grocery stores. The melons were at least eighteen inches long and full of seeds. Dad would cut a slice for each of us, and Mom said we had two choices.

We could remain at our place at the kitchen table and daintily pick out each seed with a fork, or we could go outside and spit the seeds as far as possible. Naturally, we bolted for the door.

It was exciting to see who could spit the farthest. My sister had an innate ability to chew the melon while simultaneously pushing the seeds to one side of her mouth. When she commanded "fire," Ed and I blew out one seed. Jude blew out a mouthful, one at a time. We stared in wonder as the seeds kept coming. We laughed as our sister entertained us. There was no doubt she had inherited the Kennedy wit and the love of playing pranks.

Dad often joined our seed spitting contest, but even he was no match for Jude. One thing he did demand was that we eat the watermelon right down to the rind. I remember one time when our Dafter cousins were visiting. The boys threw their rinds away with about a half-inch of melon still attached. Dad was easy-going but he was not pleased with his nephews. He said it was a house rule that the melon be consumed down to the rind instead of wasted.

I miss the wonderfully sweet watermelons of old. They were full of seeds and provided entertainment for country kids. Independence Day just isn't the same without an eighteen-inch watermelon, a seed spitting contest, and a box of simple sparklers.

The Night Dad Drank Peroxide

Recently, I discovered a jar of Swan's Powdered Boric Acid in a dark corner underneath my kitchen sink. It cost forty-nine cents and bore no UPC code because it was purchased sometime during the middle of the 20th century. I have lots of recollections of my youth, but boric acid, powdered or otherwise, is not one of them. A close inspection of the label said it was a local anti-infective for external use only and must be kept out of the reach of children. If accidentally ingested, it was important to call the local Poison Control Center. I wonder if we even had such a center in Sault Ste. Marie. I know for sure we didn't have one in Brimley during my youth. I doubt if there's even one in the whole of Chippewa County today.

In the old days, we didn't have a plethora of medicines to choose from. If we complained of a bellyache, our mother gave us an Alka-Seltzer dropped in a glass of warm water. At some point, Pepto Bismol came into use. Perhaps there were a few other stomach soothers, but I don't remember them.

I do recall one story Mom told us the morning after the event. She said Dad started coughing during the night so she reached for the bottle of cough syrup on the nightstand. There were two bottles on the stand. She didn't bother to turn on the light. In her sleepy state, she picked up one bottle and handed it to him. He took a swig, started coughing harder, and began foaming at the mouth.

Mom was immediately fully awake and turned on the light. As foam formed around Dad's mouth, she realized she had handed him the bottle of peroxide that was next to the cough syrup. No permanent damage was done, but from then on whenever Dad wanted something from the nightstand, he got it himself. He teased Mom endlessly about the night she almost did him in.

Bring Back the Barnyard

Every now and then I see something that stirs a memory. Recently I went for a drive and chanced upon a barnyard that closely resembled ours from years ago. Cows meandered around rusty machinery, a junk truck, and a lopsided hay wagon. There were piles of slab wood waiting to be buzzed. A collection of miscellaneous farming equipment stood ready for action, not knowing its usefulness had expired with the last century.

I was so intrigued by the sight I slowed down to savor it. I half-expected to see Dad driving his Case tractor with a set of disks hitched behind it. I didn't really think Dad had risen from the Great Beyond, but you know what I mean. Farms like the one I saw are quickly disappearing. Oldsters die, their land is sold, and double-wide trailers, now called manufactured homes, spring up like mushrooms. Pastures have turned into pristine lawns.

Some folks might think a junky barnyard is an eyesore, but I don't because it reminds me of bygone days. The family farm used to be an essential part of life in America. The sound of a bell echoing as the lead cow led the way from the pasture to the barn for the morning milking was a welcome sound. The rat-a-tat-tat of a tractor signaled the beginning of a farmer's work day. The sweet smell of freshly baled hay meant the mow would be filled to the rafters, and livestock would have the assurance of winter feed.

Our area has seen an influx of Amish families. A few evenings ago I was surprised to see a horse-drawn buggy going down my road. Usually they don't venture this far from the conclave on Six Mile Road. The Amish are a throwback to the old days with one major exception. Their barnyards lack the piles of junk, rolls of rusty barbed wire, and abandoned cars scattered among the clover and wildflowers. Their buildings are precision-made without a trace of torn tarpaper flapping in the wind. Tourists would be hard pressed to know the difference between their homes and ours.

Don't get me wrong. I don't yearn for the old days. I don't miss rolls of flypaper hanging from our ceilings or carrying pails of water from the wellhouse to our kitchen. I certainly don't miss the trip to the outhouse. I don't want to cook summer meals on a hot woodstove. And the last thing I want to do is trade my HP computer for an electric Adler typewriter.

But seeing that junky barnyard was a reminder of the past. For a few minutes I was transported back to the carefree days of my childhood when I could drive an abandoned car and not worry about putting play in the steering wheel or wearing out the clutch.

What's Hiding Underneath That Bale?

A Sunday afternoon drive during the summer is a treat for my eyes. If you've ever lived on a farm, you know what I mean. Take the right roads and they'll lead to fields of grass waiting to be cut or gigantic bales waiting to be wrapped and sent south. Although most small farms have disappeared, growing hay is still a good business for some local farmers. Whether square or round, small or large, their hayfields are a beautiful sight. Looking at the bales resting undisturbed beneath a sunny sky belies the amount of work that went into that idyllic scene.

Years ago the fields around my road were dotted with small, round bales. One of my chores was to accompany my sister into our hayfield and turn the bales. We did this by kicking them until the underside was exposed, thus giving it a chance to dry. Like almost everything else around our farm, this job scared me. It wasn't the difficulty in turning the bale that bothered me. It was the fear of a mouse running up my leg as the bale rolled over, and the mouse lost its hiding place.

I suppose if a professional analyst had questioned me, he would have diagnosed my condition as extreme paranoia or an unrealistic phobia. The possibility of a mouse being underneath a bale of hay was very likely. However, the fear of it running up my pant leg was highly unlikely. A mouse usually scurried away as fast as possible. It had no intention of going vertical when a horizontal exit was the most expedient and probably the safest. Like most phobias, mine was the result of an actual occurrence in the hayfield. Although a mouse did not run up my leg, it did run across my shoe. It only happened once, but once was enough to scare me forever.

Recently I had the opportunity to see men as they drove tractors pulling machinery that turned cut grass into neat, square bales. Not once did I give a thought to rodents, but I did think of old-time farmers who walked their fields, a scythe in hand, and labored for months so their animals would have winter feed. Much has changed since those days, but one thing has remained constant—the sweet aroma of a freshly mowed hayfield is delightful to inhale.

Turn off the Overhead

When I was young, Friday night was designated as the time to shop for groceries. Dad parked the car behind Callaghan's Market. Mom got out her list while my siblings and I headed down Ashmun Street to the dimestores, either Scotts or Kresge's. We usually had a dollar to spend any way we chose. In those days we could buy an ice cream soda and a toasted tuna fish sandwich and still have enough money left for candy.

I don't remember why but on the ride home one of us would turn on the overhead light. Dad would tell us to turn it off because he couldn't see. It always baffled us kids why the road suddenly disappeared when the light came on. We couldn't figure out what the light inside the car had to do with the road outside. Dad knew the way home better than we did because he traveled the same route every day when he went to work.

But in olden times kids didn't question everything as they do now. If a parent said "turn off the overhead" that's what we did. We might have pouted if we had dropped a piece of candy and had to wait until we got home to find it, but we didn't argue with our parents or challenge what they said. Once home, we helped carry in the groceries before we hunted for our Tootsie Roll, Squirrel Nut Zipper, or Root Beer Barrel. An argument only ensued if Jude or Ed found the candy I had dropped before I did and claimed it as their own.

Sometimes it takes years to understand the people who raised us. They didn't have the time, patience, or energy to sit down and explain every rule or request. We took it for granted that whatever they wanted us to do was for our benefit or the safety of ourselves and the family. Even if we didn't understand why we had to do something or not do it, we were obedient. Perhaps things were done differently at our house. I don't know how other parents treated their children, but we had it pretty easy.

Turning off the overhead light was not a monumental task, nor did it involve anything more strenuous than reaching for the dome and pushing the switch or whatever it took to turn off the light. It wasn't painful or an attack on our self-esteem. We didn't feel belittled or picked on. We knew we had no business turning that light on in the first place.

To this day I follow the old rule. I rarely drive at night but when I do I wouldn't dream of turning on the overhead to find something I dropped. I wait until I get home to search for it. Dad would be pleased.

Landing in the Poor House

As a kid I remember hearing adults talking about "landing in the poor house." When I was upstairs playing with my dolls, I listened to whatever was being said below. The stovepipe ran from the kitchen through my playroom so it wasn't like I was snooping on purpose. I had no option. If I had left the room every time the adults conversed, my dolls would have thought I had abandoned them.

Christmas is when the poor house was mentioned the most, but it wasn't the voice of my mother I heard. It was that of an old neighbor who lived alone and somehow managed to exist without an income. Regardless of the weather, he walked to our house almost every day. Dad always had a chore for him and gave him a few dollars. Mom invited him to stay for a meal. If he refused, she put food in a sack and he took it home. When he left, my parents discussed how to keep him from the dreaded poor house.

As a youngster I pictured it as a place where adults went when they ran out of money. I thought they were treated the same as Mr. Scrooge treated Mr. Cratchit. I wasn't sure where the house was in the Soo, but I thought it might be next to the Emma Nason home on Ashmun. That's where orphans went so it made sense to me that their parents would be next door. Every time we went to town, we passed the Nason home and I hoped the little kids got to see their mom and dad at least once a year on Christmas day.

Children have an innate ability to imagine all sorts of things from snatches of conversations they overhear. In those days we weren't allowed to give our opinions on anything. We didn't ask questions and if we did the responses we received were probably lies to soften the truth. If I had asked what would happen if our neighbor landed in the poor house, most likely I would have been told he would be given good food, a blanket, and a cot. That would have satisfied my curiosity.

Even as a child, I felt sorry for poor people. I didn't think we were poor because we had everything we needed. Dad had a job. We had a car. We lived in a house. We had lots of food. We had cows in the barn and hay in the mow. We had school clothes, church clothes, and everyday clothes that might have patches on the knees but were good enough. We had barn clothes. My sister had movie magazines. My brother had cowboy toys. I had dolls plus a collection of Little Golden Books neatly arranged in an orange crate bookcase. Stories like *A Christmas Carol* filled in the gaps of my limited knowledge of poverty.

Just before Christmas, Mom gave our destitute neighbor a box full of gifts that included lots of food and a can of tobacco. In my childish way, I thought my parents were helping him avoid the poor house while simultaneously teaching us the true meaning of Christmas, a lesson my siblings and I never forgot. Even at a young age, I equated wealth with sharing what we had with others. Although I never did find out where the Soo's poor house was, our neighbor escaped being carted off to it. He lived to a ripe old age in his tarpaper shack, and my parents continued to show him kindness and charity until he went to that beautiful house in the sky where all good people go when they die.

The Lost Art of Ironing

The other day I finally got around to washing my summer pillowcases and white percale sheets. They've been in my linen closet since September so I thought I would freshen them up before I put them on my bed. As I ran the iron over them, I was reminded of the days of my youth when I couldn't wait to learn how to iron. There was something magical about the way that hot metal triangle glided over whatever Mom put on the padded wooden board.

The summer I was nine, she agreed it was time I learned the art of getting wrinkles out of dishtowels, hankies, and pillowcases. Mom was my drill sergeant, standing guard over me and giving strict instructions on how to avoid burning myself as well as whatever I was ironing. She watched in terror as I picked up the heavy Sunbeam, dipped my fingers in a jar filled with water, and flicked the iron to see if a hiss told me it was hot enough to begin my task.

I took to ironing like a baker takes to bread. When Mom was sure I wasn't going to burn a hole in her monogrammed pillowcases or fancy lace hankies, she went back to her kitchen chores. The ironing board was nearby so she kept a sharp eye on my progress while she baked a cake or fixed our lunch. The radio was always tuned to WSOO and Mom hummed or sang as she worked. I did likewise.

I still remember the sweet fragrance of line-dried dishtowels when they came in contact with the hot iron. I took great care to straighten the edges and unfurl the hems if needed. I ironed one side and then the other whether it was necessary or not. I folded and pressed, folded and pressed until Dad's hankies were the size of a neat two-inch square. When I reached for a delicate hanky, I made the last fold triangular, then turned each end toward the middle. Every move I made was based on what I had seen my mother do many times as she took the wash from the laundry basket and ironed it.

Mom's sister, Marie, knew how to monogram. She lived in Detroit and worked for a monogram company until she bought a machine, made patterns, and started her own business. We had monogrammed shirts, blouses, towels, skirts, hankies, sheets, and pillowcases. Aunt Marie wrote our names on everything. Even Dad had his name on his work clothes. But what I loved most were the pillowcases. Those large white cotton ones were beautiful.

Recently a flood of memories came over me as I ironed items with pink crocheting around the edges and pink and blue flowers on the hem. The ones Aunt Marie made for Mom and Dad have "Mr." and "Mrs." written in green thread alongside a green house. They were a wedding present. Mom never used them, but every few years I wash them, hang them on the outside line, iron them, and put them away until the next time I repeat the process.

When I was in high school, I ironed much more than tea towels and pillowcases. As I graduated to clothing, some of the thrill of ironing left me, but I was still proud of the finished products. I made many of my own clothes and my skill with an iron came in handy by lending a professional look to my garments. Even when polyester and other synthetic materials hit the market, I still preferred cotton. To this day, ironing is a task I enjoy while listening to the radio.

I know it sounds crazy to get sentimental over something as insignificant as ironing a pillowcase, but that's often the way it is when we grow old. We remember the times when things were made in America and when a clothesline was in every yard. We remember making our own steam by sprinkling water on whatever was taken from the clothes basket. We remember the clean, fresh smell of a summer day as we guided our iron down a long-sleeved shirt or around the intricate collar of a blouse. We remember the feeling of accomplishment when the work was done and everything was hung on hangers or neatly stacked and ready to be put in a drawer or on a shelf.

Today most clothes are thrown in the washer and dryer or left in a plastic basket until needed. There's no rhythm to the chore. No mystery. With the exception of a few choice articles, the clothes of most teenagers are tossed helter-skelter with no respect for the effort it took to make them. There's no ironing or mending them, and no connection with the person who made them.

Last week when I was checking my wellhouse to see how it had survived the winter, I saw the little wooden ironing board and red electric iron from my childhood. In today's world, I can't imagine any parent giving such Christmas gifts to their daughter, but my presents stood as silent witnesses to a little girl who loved to iron. I thought about putting the items in my garage sale, but changed my mind. I think I'll keep them a few more years as a reminder of my sweet, simple past.

The Fields of My Father

On New Year's Day 2019 I strapped cleats to my boots and walked down the road. I passed forty acres that once belonged to Dad. Then I walked past my brother's house to another field of Dad's. I stopped for a few minutes and surveyed all that once had been so active when he was alive. I looked at old machinery standing silent, heedless of snowflakes slowly drifting down, threatening to blanket the hay wagons and seeders and fill the manure spreader with a layer of snow.

Being the sentimental fool I am, tears filled my eyes. I wondered what Dad would think if he could see the field in need of brushing and the farm equipment rusting and sinking deeper into the ground. The tractor he had used in all seasons was safely in a shed, but the rest of his machinery was waiting for its master to return and put it to good use. But not being human, the rakes and wagons, combine and seeder could only wait for that time which will never come again.

I thought about the summer Dad took hay off the field where I was standing. I remembered it because it was the one and only time I drove the Case. I don't know what was hitched to the tractor, but Dad walked alongside it and cautioned me about turning too sharply when I made the turn at the end of the field. That's all I remember. Everything else is forgotten except Dad telling me to be careful.

Some memories are like that. They're permanently embedded in our mind. We don't even know we remember them until we see or hear something that brings them back to us. I looked at the trees surrounding the field and the tracks of jack rabbits and deer. I saw the trail where I had snowshoed earlier in the week. I thought of Malcolm, a faithful canine pet, whose unmarked grave was somewhere in the field. I thought of all the things that once were but are now gone, and I was sad. Then, as if on cue, the sun broke through the clouds and a song came to my lips. It was an old tune and I recalled only a few lines, but I stood in Dad's field and sang what I remembered.

As crazy as this sounds, I sang to the trees, the snow, the animals, the machinery, and to the past and present and to all that was and still is. You know what I mean, because sometimes you sing when no one hears you except your empty rooms or the field of your father's. You sing because if you don't, your heart will break with yearning for those who are no more.

Part VI:
An Oldster's
Viewpoint

There's Rain in Them Thair Clouds

I never dreamed I'd utter the same words my grandmother used to say when the sky clouded up and threatened rain. Arthritis caused her hands to ache, and she knew a downpour wasn't far off. Of course, I didn't believe her. In my young mind, nobody could predict the weather by the pain in their bones. Whoever heard of such a silly thing?

Well, fast forward and you know perfectly well who. In 1998, I broke my ankle in two places. I didn't cry until I saw the X-rays. My poor little bones were dangling by a thread. The doctor took one look and said he would pin and plate them. When I told him I didn't have health insurance, he never missed a beat. He said a cast would be just fine. He wrapped and plastered and sent me home, telling me to keep off my feet for six weeks. I spent all those weeks on my back. I hired someone to cut the grass. I asked another Avon lady to deliver my orders. A friend brought groceries and washed our clothes. My daughter acted as nursemaid. Another friend planted the oak seedlings I had ordered a few weeks prior to my fall. Everyone was kind and helpful.

It took a long time for my ankle to predict the weather. Maybe some bones are smarter than others, I don't know, but my bones didn't wise up for at least ten years. Even then it didn't occur to me that the ache in my ankle meant rain. I didn't immediately connect the two until a few years ago so I guess I'm just as dumb as my bones. Last week, the sky opened up and rain poured down in buckets. By 8:00 a.m. my back yard had a number of little ponds, my front yard looked like a small lake, and my leaky garage was about to float away. As for my ankle, it did what mended, arthritic ankles are supposed to do. It ached. It throbbed. It caused me discomfort, and it did all this long before one tiny drop of rain had fallen from the clouds.

So there you have it. What was bizarre and foreign to me as a child has now become commonplace. Some oldsters probably know what I mean. If you predict the weather by the ache in your bones, your grandchildren might think you're losing your marbles. I can only imagine the look of surprise on a child's face when rain falls on cue. It's nice to know our bones only let us down when they break. Otherwise, they're often more accurate than the weatherman.

A Sink Divided

The first time I washed dishes in a divided sink was exciting. There was no sink in the home of my youth, only a white enamel dishpan and a large galvanized rinse pan. I'm reaching way back in my memory, but I think we usually left the dishpan on the woodstove when we washed the dishes. We transferred them to the rinse pan which we probably carried to the kitchen table. The dishpan might have been on the table, too, if the stove was so hot the water would have burned our hands. I simply don't remember.

At times I had washed dishes in my uncle's sink, but it wasn't divided. It was the old style, deep and long. A divided sink was modern and solved two issues. There was no need for a separate rinse pan and no worry that the sink would overflow due to the amount of rinse water added to it. True, both sides of the sink were small when compared to a "farmhouse" sink, but that was of little concern to me. When my folks bought this Marlette mobile home, the green sink with two sides was undoubtedly the most splendid thing I had ever seen.

You can't imagine how wonderful it was to put dishes in one side of our new sink and rinse them in the other. It was equally delightful to turn a tap and have hot and cold water on command. No need to take the empty water pails to the wellhouse, turn on the pump, fill the pails, and carry them back to the house. No need to fill the dishpan with cold water and wait for it to heat on the woodstove, but even with the new sink we kept the same washing routine that had begun long before my birth. The first items we plunged into the hot, soapy water were glasses, then cups and saucers, then plates and silverware. Pots and pans went in last. Of course, the cast iron frying pans never saw the inside of a dishpan or a sink. That would have destroyed their well-seasoned interior.

After we finished our first meal in our new home, I volunteered to wash the dishes. Mom nearly fainted because dishwashing was low on my list of favorite chores. I filled the sink with hot water and squirted in a good dose of dishwashing liquid. It might have been Palmolive, but I could be mistaken. What I'm not mistaken about is the first glass I broke as I was transferring it from the right side of the sink to the left side. The wonderful divider got in the way. I wasn't used to such a marvelous piece of engineering and didn't lift the glass high enough to avoid a collision. That broken glass was the first of many. It didn't take Mom long to suggest I stick to making the beds and leave the washing of dishes to her.

I still use the same sink today. I'm just a lot more careful. Mom would be proud.

The Broken Cup

As a creature of habit, every morning I use the same coffee cup. It's a small one that barely holds six ounces. I refill it three times. The caffeine helps me get up and get going. Larger mugs are in my cupboard, but I avoid them. There's something about a twelve or sixteen ounce mug with a half-inch lip that I find disgusting. I like my coffee hot. If it's in a cup the size of a cereal bowl, it's cold by the time I reach the remaining inch and about as appetizing as a bottle of pop that lost its fizz.

A few weeks ago I was drying my favorite cup when it slipped from my hands, fell to the floor, and broke into three pieces. Well, I thought, that's the end of that. As I swept the shards into the dustpan and threw them in the recycling container, I wondered where I could find another small coffee cup. I rarely shop at resale stores or garage sales, the most likely places to discover what I wanted. Then I had an epiphany. If there was one kitchen cupboard in the whole of the U.P. that held the perfect cup, it was my brother's. Before the day was over, I walked down the road and raided his cupboard. I brought home a new, albeit used, vessel for my coffee. Order had been restored and all was well in my little world. If all our troubles could be solved as easily as replacing a broken cup, our cares would be few. Unfortunately, this is rarely the case.

The longer we live the more broken things we encounter that can never be repaired with a dab of glue or the help of a brother. Problems come our way that chip at our self-esteem and leave cracks so deep they never heal. As a china cup riddled with glaze crackles can harbor unseen bacteria so, too, microscopic cracks in our life can have devastating results. A cracked cup isn't strong enough to withstand hot liquid. A broken soul is often too weak to withstand the rigors of daily life.

Cracks and chips in cups are obvious, but fissures and emotional fractures seared into the core of an individual are often disguised by smiles and laughter. Sometimes the only way a broken person can survive is by pretense. Glazing over wounds is a normal tactic for some people who suffer from an unseen illness. There's no quick cure for loneliness or heartache or disappointment. These may seem like trivial ailments, but to the one who endures them, they can be lethal. Call my broken cup a metaphor for life or merely a topic for this column. Either way, I'm ready for my second dose of java in my borrowed six ounce cup.

The Mystery of the Disappearing Bar of Soap

The other day I was squirting liquid soap on my hands as I washed them in the bathroom sink. That small gesture got me thinking about years ago when our soap dish held an orange bar of Lifebuoy. We all used it. Dad when he washed up after doing the barn chores. Mom when she was going to a PTA meeting. We kids scrubbed the daily grime from our face, neck, ears, and hands without giving the bar a second thought. The amazing thing is we all survived each other's germs.

When Mom brought home our first bar of Ivory, I was awestruck. I couldn't imagine how soap could float. It was a magical phenomenon unheard of in my little world. Ivory smelled nice, too, not like the medicinal odor of Lifebuoy and a whole lot better than the Fels-Neptha Mom used to scrub the stains out of our clothes.

We didn't have a regular bathroom in our house, but we did have a washstand. It was a piece of furniture Dad nailed together. I have no idea what the top was made of because Mom covered it with yellow checked oilcloth held in place with thumbtacks. In those days, just about everything was secured with a couple of tacks—the calendars that covered our walls, the oilcloth on the pantry table, even the trim on a fancy wooden chair. A small, white granite pan and a saucer that held a bar of soap were stationary items on our washstand. I don't remember when Mom bought our first official soap dish, but I'm sure we made a fuss about it. In the old days, country kids got excited about things now considered trivial. Who cares about a fancy dish for a bar of soap? Well, we did. At least I think we did. How much trivia can one brain retain without going wacky?

Well anyway, when I go shopping I always feel a little guilty when I reach for liquid soap instead of Camay or Zest or whichever bar soap I would usually put in my cart. It took me a long time to purchase the liquid stuff. I cling to traditions of the past like a burr clings to clothing. When a friend gave me some expensive liquid soap guaranteed to kill all bacteria, I used it to scrub my toilet. When a niece splashed out cash for a bottle of good smelling stuff from Bath & Body, I splashed it all over my tub. The corker came when a friend visited and chastised me for not getting with the times.

You know you're licked when an old bachelor gives you the dickens over a bar of soap. Willy pointed out all the dangers inherent in sharing the same bar. Why, he said, it would be like sharing the same toothbrush or fork or towel. When I told him there was only one hand towel in my bathroom, I thought his heart would give out. I explained I'm the only one who uses it, but Willy was undeterred. He asked what if a visitor stopped by and wiped her feet on my towel. Would I want to use it on my face? I told him my lady friends had more sense than to do something as stupid as that and asked what kind of friends he had. But after he left, I caved. The next time I went shopping, I bought two hand towels and something I never had any intention of purchasing. I bought my first bottle of colored liquid gel at the dollar store.

I refused to pay more than $1 for something I didn't want and felt pressured into buying. It stood next to my soap dish for at least a week before I twisted the top and popped up the squirter thingy. I had to admit it was more convenient than my bar soap, and it was a whole lot faster. Those extra seconds I saved could be added to my Netflix watching time. It was neater, too, and I didn't have to worry about water in the soap dish, or conversely, a bar getting old and stiff if it wasn't used too often. I didn't want to admit it, but I was hooked.

It's an awful thing to forsake tradition. It's turning your back on the old and embracing the new. It's a rejection of the true and trusted and a leap of faith into the unknown. I know it's only soap, but that's how new things creep into our lives. Before we know it, our socks become dust rags, our buttons are replaced with Velcro, our oxfords give way to Reeboks, and our bandanas are tucked in a drawer and forgotten.

But I'll tell you a secret. Behind my shower curtain is a yellow plastic soap dish with a fresh bar of Olay in it. I'm still clinging to tradition like that stubborn old burr clings to a pair of green polyester work pants.

Three Cheers for Pond's

About two months ago, I used the last of my expensive facial night cream. I don't like to use the day cream at night because it has SPF in it, and I can assure you there's no sunlight in my bedroom past 9:00 p.m. so there's no fear of getting sunburned. Anyway, I remembered the small jar of Pond's in a corner of my medicine cabinet. I dug it out and started using it. Last week I scraped the last little bit from the jar. It was only when I ran out of the expensive night cream that I realized good old Pond's was the better choice.

Many of us are fooled by slick advertising. I've given up on all the creams promising miraculous disappearance of age spots, crow's feet, and chicken necks. I never swallow concoctions guaranteed to stop the aging process, although I might give Ivermectin a try in an attempt to eradicate the lines across my forehead. First, though, I'll visit a horse farm and see if any of their old nags have facial wrinkles. I wouldn't want to subject my system to anything that might backfire and give me a result I wasn't expecting.

I guess I've reached an age when I'm too tired to give much thought to anything other than humor. Yes, occasionally I write a serious column, but I've been serious all my life and I'm tired of it. My sister always saw the funny side of things. My perception of everything was tragic. She wasn't much of a reader, but if she had been, she would have enjoyed Shakespeare's comedies while I devoured his tragedies. Raised in the same house with the same parents, we were as different as sugar and salt.

Sometimes the good old remedies are the best. You know what I mean because you still rub Vicks on your chest when you have a cold, still keep a jar of Vaseline handy for cuts and scrapes, and still drop an Alka-Seltzer in tepid water when your tummy aches. Bag Balm has moved from the barn where it was used to soften a cow's milk dispensers and is now considered an effective moisturizer for humans. Mane 'n Tail is sold alongside Paul Mitchell and other outrageously expensive shampoos.

I'm awaiting the day when catnip will be used to arouse women who always complain of a headache at bedtime. Milk-Bones will move from the doggy's dish, whizzed into powder, mixed with a speck of water, and used as toothpaste. After all, if those bones remove tartar from Fido's teeth, surely they'll do the same for ours. A quick Google search found the most effective growth hormone in cattle is Somatotropin. If we want more meat and less fat on our bones, maybe we should order a sample from an Internet site.

And so it goes. From Pond's to steroids, from the sensible to the absurd, Jude was right. Life really is a ridiculous, laughable, merry-go-round. Grab a horse and jump on.

Getting Shanghaied

Now I know why Mom shanghaied anyone who spent more than five minutes at her kitchen table. Whenever someone dropped by, she immediately handed them a list of chores that needed attention. Mom was a widow so much of what Dad would have done was left undone when he was gone. She was capable of shoveling a path through the snow to the garage, cutting grass throughout the summer, or moving the burn barrel from one spot to another, but some things were just too difficult. As soon as a visitor finished his tea, he was put to work.

Having lived alone for many years, I, too, find myself following Mom's example. I shanghai anyone who crosses my threshold. It doesn't matter who it is. It might be a neighbor stopping by to ask if I've seen his cat. Nope, but how about making a sign for my garage sale. Or perhaps a stranger calls and wants me to autograph a copy of my book. Sure, I'll oblige him right after he's shoveled the snow from my roofs and changed the oil in my car. Yes, friend, you may have the free firewood, but only after you've promised to dig up six white pines and transplant them in my front yard.

See what I mean? I've become my mother and perfected the art of shanghaiing. On one hand, living alone is great because we don't have to answer to anyone. On the other hand, it's not so great when there's work to be done and we can't do it. It's either too hard or we lack the necessary knowledge, skill, equipment, or strength. Recently the UPS man stopped by with a delivery. As soon as I saw his truck, I raced down my vestibule steps. I had a job for him that had nothing to do with the package he was dropping off. I asked him if he would mind doing a tiny little favor for me that would only take a minute. All he had to do was step inside and remove the water filter from my kitchen tap. My hand wasn't strong enough to loosen it. He hesitated but I looked so pitiful he agreed. He unscrewed the old filter and put in the new one in less time than it took to write this column.

A friend has a small utility trailer hitched behind his truck. Over the years, I've shanghaied him into moving lots of stuff from one place to another and doing various other chores. He showed up one day last summer when I wasn't home, but he knew the routine and set to work. By the time I returned, he had put new string in my weed whacker and was busy whacking every weed in sight. Before he left, he mentioned there was a wasp nest near my wishing well. I felt a momentary twinge of guilt because he had been stung a few times. To ease my conscience, I offered him a squirt of Bactine.

So if you're heading in my direction by all means stop in and say hello. However, before entering my dwelling grab the snow shovel. And come summer make sure you wear old clothes when you visit me. You know what's coming after you've consumed the last cookie and your teacup is empty.

Reaching for a Fork

The other day I made a kale, brown rice, and quinoa casserole. I added a few vegetables, various seasonings, and a cheddar cheese sauce. Then I topped it with cubes of homemade bread. When I took it from the oven, I dished some into a bowl and reached for a spoon. Then I came to my senses. Am I a two-year-old I asked myself. What am I doing with a spoon? Immediately I got out my favorite fork.

Folks who live alone will understand when I say there's one fork I prefer over the others. Three summers ago I sold two complete sets of flatware for twelve but kept three mismatched teaspoons, three butter knives, two soup spoons, one ice tea spoon, and four forks. My favorite fork is one I've had for more than thirty years. It's the only one I use. The tines on the newer ones are too long, the forks are too heavy, and the designs are too modern. I prefer the shape, style, and comfort of my old fork.

Comfort from a fork? I know what you're thinking. You're shaking your head and saying Kennedy is losing her marbles. You're thinking perhaps you should contact my brother or daughter and suggest they have me committed. Sharon's lived alone too long, you're saying to a friend. She talks about a cat that talks to her. She walks down the road during snowstorms. She dresses like a bag lady. She doesn't own a microwave, a Keurig coffee maker, a tablet, or a cell phone. She's a hopeless recluse and now she's saying a fork gives her comfort? Call the authorities.

Well, wait a minute. Apply the brakes. Obviously, if any reader agrees with what I've just said, you're not old and you don't live alone. You haven't yet acquired the quirks and idiosyncrasies that solitary old age gives you. You're not set in your ways. You're still pliable. There's hope for you. There's the possibility you're willing to change to accommodate a partner, a spouse, or even a cat. You grab the nearest fork regardless of its size and weight. You use a regular teaspoon instead of an ice tea spoon to stir milk into your cereal. Any old butter knife will do when you spread jam on your toast. Bravo for you. You're in the flush of youth.

But here's a news flash. Old age is coming. It's nipping at your heels and no matter how fast you run, you can't outrun it. One day you, too, will have a favorite fork, sweater, or purse you won't let go of. The tines might be bent, moths might have attacked the sweater, and the purse might be held together with safety pins, but none of that will matter. Why? Because these things will give you comfort.

I rest my case.

An Endless Supply of Tears

Recently I was watching a documentary about a young person who touched the lives of many although he wasn't given long on this earth. As often happens when I watch something that pulls at my heartstrings, tears filled my eyes. It was then I decided to write about our endless supply of tears. No matter how many we shed throughout our lifetime, there's always a full supply in our invisible stockpile.

We cry when we're happy and we cry when we're sad. We weep at births, christenings, graduations, weddings, and funerals. Sometimes we laugh until we cry. Other times it's a song or a fragrance that brings tears to our eyes. We sob when our partner leaves us, and we sob even harder when he comes back. We wail when our dog dies. We brush aside tears when we watch a good movie or read a book that touches us. We're sad when loved ones move away, and cry tears of joy if they return.

Although I have no proof, I have a theory that holidays are responsible for many tears. Perhaps the spiked eggnog or mulled cider has something to do with it, or maybe it's all those Christmas carols that stir up sadness. Regardless of what triggers them, tears gush forth like Old Faithful. But where do they come from? I've often said I've shed enough tears to fill Lake Erie and yet they still keep coming. I don't get it. I don't even like crying. I never cried as a kid. It was drilled into me not to wear my heart on my sleeve so I took my lumps, kept my mouth shut, and hardened my heart. Well, I hardened it towards mean people but not towards animals. An animal acts out of instinct. People often act out of envy.

But at one time or another everyone cries, even the hardest and most despicable among us. It amazes and confounds me that from the cradle to the grave, tears are the one unchanging constant. Whether newborn or minutes from our final exit, our tear storehouse is always full. Everything else in our physical realm is likely to go haywire. Our body stoops and sags as we age. Our eyes and ears give out. Our joints get rusty. Our teeth and hair give up and fall out. Our memory catches a glimpse of the past, and we think we're still young.

I've learned a few things about this crying business. Number one is, we'll run out of energy but we'll never out of tears. Secondly, they change nothing. Thirdly, the quicker they come to our eyes, the more compassionate we tend to be. And finally, they're good for the economy. Without us crybabies, Kleenex and Puffs would have gone bust years ago. Something to ponder as you reach for a tissue.

Clinging to Dignity as the Years Pass

As we age it often gets harder to cling to our dignity. For some folks, losing a sense of dignity is due to major health problems that require constant medical attention including poking and probing into our physical body. For others, it's dealing with ailments like arthritis, knee problems, and poor vision. Regardless of the cause, having to admit we need help can be difficult for those of us who have always been independent. Something as simple as opening a jar of pickles can cause frustration when our hands no longer have the strength to twist off the lid. Even if we're alone in the kitchen and no one sees us, we feel ourselves slipping into that gray zone called old age. I remember my grandmother asking me to thread a needle for her. I was just a little girl and was surprised Gram couldn't see the hole and slide the thread through it. Now I understand.

What bothers me most about losing my youth is realizing it's never coming back. For the past few years, I've avoided driving at night because my vision is poor. The result is I've missed attending events I would have enjoyed. I'm too proud to ask a friend to take me. Just because we're friends doesn't mean we like the same things. Living on a sideroad doesn't help either. Our road is always icy in winter. I wouldn't want someone to slide into the ditch or hit a deer on their way to my place. Imagine the guilt I'd feel.

Dignity is one of those rare qualities in our modern world, but for oldsters it was something we always took for granted. As girls, we dressed modestly, practiced good manners, and tried our best to act like young ladies. Fellows didn't cuss in front of us or tell crude jokes. Siblings argued back and forth, but it went no further than bickering over a candy bar or television show. It was harmless and left no permanent emotional scars.

Despite all our advances in technology, psychology, and peer relationships, it seems many youths and adults of today have slid down the dignity ladder. Is it just us old fogies who cling to our dignity like that proverbial clinging burr I often mention? Perhaps we want to be called Ma'am. Perhaps we want doors opened for us, and when we dine out we certainly appreciate a nice, clean restaurant.

That's not to say we want to be coddled as if we were an organic egg, but we do want to be treated with respect and some semblance of dignity. We are well aware the niceties of our younger days are slipping away, but that's no reason for us to fall in line and accept modern behavior. I suppose young people don't understand us any more than we understand them. It's more than just a generation gap. It's a cultural gulf that some of us may never cross.

Growing old means facing a lot of challenges. Some are easier to accept than others. We might be willing to walk with a cane, but no one wants to wear Depends. Sometimes we drop things due to arthritic hands, but we don't want our house to smell like Watkins Liniment. We don't mind losing a back molar, but dread the thought of a complete set of new choppers. We agree to visit the doctor twice a year for a checkup, but cringe at the thought of a serious illness.

We cling to whatever dignity we have left because we know it will disappear if we end up in a nursing home so take my advice. Hold your head high as you walk with a cane while wearing Depends. Dine at a fancy restaurant and hope your teeth don't fall out with your first bite. And if sickness comes your way, fight it with all the strength of a rhinoceros.

Ode to the Wooden Icebox

During the winter storm of 2020, my electricity was off for three days. Luckily I didn't have anything in the freezer compartment of my refrigerator except two trays of ice cubes, four cans of "frozen" cranberry juice, a box of puff pastry, and a bag of organic flax seed. With the exception of the iffy pastry, the rest of the stuff survived the outage.

But as the days waned and I watched darkness descend, I wondered how long the power would be out. Because there was nothing else to do, I started reflecting on the past when folks weren't dependent upon a mysterious grid to keep things going. Women did their evening mending by the light of a kerosene lamp. Men did the milking by lantern light. They had stoves that burned wood, cows that gave milk, a root cellar to store vegetables from their garden, a hand pump to bring water up from the well, and a wooden icebox to keep things cold. During winter, men cut through the frozen lakes and loaded chunks of ice onto a wagon pulled by horses. Once home, the ice was stored in a shed or "ice house." The ice was covered with sawdust as an insulator and brought in when the ice in the kitchen icebox had melted into the drip pan. I'm not sure when our icebox was replaced by a refrigerator, but I do remember playing with the former when it was moved to the wellhouse, the second room of which was my playhouse.

By the time I was old enough to know the difference between a metal box and an oak one, I didn't care. All I knew was I liked the white box better because it was easier to open than the door that had latches. Ice cream lasted longer than five minutes, and there was no drip pan to be emptied twice a day.

Thinking about the old days made me wonder what my grandparents would say about our total dependence upon the grid. I don't own a gas-powered generator. When the lights go out at my place so go the range, furnace, Internet, radio, television, answering machine, water pump, and any hope of flushing the toilet. All I can do is light a candle, wrap a comforter around me, and wait for the linemen to find the problem and restore power.

Do I want to return to the days of the icebox? No, but I wish I could survive without depending upon that magical grid to keep my ice cubes frozen and my puff pastry preserved. When I wrote this, a snowstorm was raging outside my windows. Such storms raged when I was young, but we had the woodstove in the kitchen and the oil stove in the front room. We also had a milk can filled with water for our drinking and cooking needs. We had numerous kerosene lamps, so surviving a three-day storm was not the problem it is today. And, need I mention, we also had the outhouse. Electricity was not required for the two-holer. There was no need for an electric pump to draw up well water and fill the toilet's tank because there wasn't one. We didn't give a hoot about something called a grid.

There's No Such Thing as a Chicken Crow

At one time or another, we've all seen a crow dining on a dead skunk or some other unlucky rodent lying in the middle of the road or alongside it. I was driving to Brimley one day and wondered if the crow on the road ahead of me would fly away before I hit it, or if this time my car would end its happy days as a scavenger. Crows play "chicken" all the time. They usually win, and Saturday was no exception. The crow flew away from his dinner seconds before he would have met his doom under one of my tires.

I don't know if crows are courageous, hungry, or just plain stupid. Why do they wait until the last minute before they head for the sky? Do they have poor eyesight and do not see a car approaching? Are they hard of hearing? Are they concentrating more on filling their belly than on their safety? I did a quick Google search and found some answers. Crows have excellent eyesight and better hearing than most humans so my first two questions were answered. Crows are also very intelligent so I suppose they're not thinking about safety. They're thinking about timing. They know the exact moment when to take flight. Unlike some of us who hang around a situation too long and end up in hot water, crows seem to possess better judgment.

It's very rare to see a dead crow on the road, but it's not uncommon to see a seagull. Those poor birds are heavier than crows, so it takes them longer to escape highway danger. And if truth be told, seagulls lack the intelligence of crows. To prove my point without conducting a longitudinal study, I'll ask a simple question. Have you ever seen a crow hopping around a fast-food restaurant parking lot? Probably not, but I'll bet you've seen seagulls begging for a bite of your Big Mac or a handful of French fries.

Some crows are like people. They stick their beaks into business other than their own. Crows are notorious for raiding nests and devouring eggs and nestlings. They have no conscience when it comes to taking something that doesn't belong to them. They make no apologies for the destruction they leave behind because that's their nature. It's also in their genetic makeup to raid compost piles and suet meant for chickadees, but undoubtedly their favorite meal is road kill. That's a good thing because crows act as maintenance keepers of the roadways. They assist the county workers without requiring any other payment than a dead porcupine or squirrel.

The sight of a crow playing chicken got me thinking. I know a fellow who drives his car with one thumb on the steering wheel. He says he has more control than most people who grip the wheel with both hands. I don't like to ride with him, but if I have to, I request he put at least one finger as well as his thumb on the wheel. Naturally, he refuses. I know another person who depends upon her brakes to compensate for her obsession with speed. She waits until the last minute to slam on the brakes to avoid crashing into the car in front of her. She whizzes down dirt roads at high speeds, totally oblivious to the possibility of a deer, dog, or any other animal crossing in front of her. When we plan an outing, I always suggest we take my car, but she says I drive like an old lady. I end up in her vehicle and endure another white-knuckle ride.

What do these two characters have in common? Obviously, they enjoy playing chicken. They're like crows. They have faith in their ability to outwit any potentially dangerous situation. They have no respect or consideration for the person in the passenger seat. They assume they're invincible and as far as I know, luck has been with them. It's not skill that has kept them from causing an accident, so it must be luck as well as timing. They give themselves just enough time to grab the wheel or slam on the brakes before impact. Maybe I'm an old fuddy-duddy, but as much as possible I avoid riding with Mr. Thumb and Mrs. Brakeaholic.

As we age, I suppose we go in one of two directions. We become more rigid and set in our ways or more pliable and accepting of change. Unlike crows, we see no reason to play chicken with life.

Go Outside and Play

In the old days, parents didn't have to tell their offspring to "go outside and play." During summer it was something we automatically did after our morning chores were done. We couldn't wait to get outside and climb trees, build forts, pick wildflowers, comb the fields for the first tiny strawberries, or grab a fishing pole and head for the river down the road. Riding our bikes was a given, even when the gravel was thick and the going was rough. Facing a strong wind was a real challenge, but it didn't stop us from biking to a friend's house. We knew the wind would be to our back when it was time to go home.

Picking wildflowers and searching for berry patches were some of my favorite summertime activities. If it was a rainy day, I had plenty of coloring books or books to read from my small library. "I'm bored" was an expression unknown to country kids when I was growing up. We knew how to make our own fun without the aid of anything more elaborate than our imagination. We had acres of fields and woods to explore any time of the year, and we had chores to do every day. I can't imagine telling my parents I was bored. Mom would have handed me a dust cloth and said get busy. Dad would have handed me a manure fork if I ventured to the barn.

After our evening chores, we were free to do whatever we wanted. For me, that meant taking a long bike ride by myself. As a teenager, I loved seeing dusk descend and watching the fog roll in. I would often hum or sing a country song as I pedaled down the road with one of the dogs by my side. Sparky was Jude's dog, but even if I told him to stay home, he paid no attention. As soon as he saw me heading for the red shed and my bicycle, he was already halfway down the lane. He was eager for one last run before nightfall.

Kids of today rarely hear their parents telling them to "go outside and play." It isn't safe. What a pity they'll never know the freedom I experienced all those decades ago when nobody gave personal safety a second thought.

Waking at Three in the Morning

Sometimes I awaken during the night and start thinking about things and wondering what will happen in the future. I don't have many sleepless nights, but when I do, I don't like them. Along with worrying about the years to come, they also stir up memories of the past that are best forgotten. We can't do anything about either, so why does our mind take us to places we'd rather not go?

You know what I mean because you also awaken at three in the morning, and your mind won't let you rest. You weep for loved ones who are no more, or for your grandchildren who face an unpredictable future. We live in precarious times. I suppose every generation has thought the same thing, but I think it's worse today. We can't escape the endless barrage of news reminding us that our world is changing, and by all accounts the future will be much worse than the past.

When we were young and carefree, we worried about nothing. The arrival of spring meant mud. Often we walked out of our boots and felt the cold, squishy earth as it turned our socks from bright white to dirty brown. Did we cry or moan? No. We laughed, because it was all part of spring, as was walking to the corner to catch the bus when the road was a muddy mess.

Spring meant the river overflowed its banks, but we weren't frightened. We knew the water couldn't climb the hill so we were safe. Spring also meant May peepers and great clumps of frog eggs in the ditches. It meant searching the fields to find arbutus, the sweetest flower of them all, so tiny yet so fragrant. We picked them for our mother as a gift that cost us nothing but an hour of our time.

We played outside all day and only came in the house for lunch. We rode our bicycles. We explored the woods behind our house. We knew the names of trees and wild flowers. We got stung by bees and rubbed mud on the sting. We stepped in cow pies as we headed for the woods to build teepees.

In the evening after our ball games, we took Mason jars and caught lightning bugs. We watched as they lit up the night and wondered how anything so small could produce such a glow. We released them before we entered the house and went to bed. Our dreams weren't of the past or future, and we slept soundly until morning.

So when you awaken at 3:00 a.m., concentrate on the present. If you're still awake when dawn breaks forth, rejoice. Welcome the new day as eagerly as you did when you were young. Don't think about what was or what will come. We can't change either. We'll just carry on as best we can.

The Passing of Summer

The timothy has gone to seed. The goldenrod is in full bloom. Queen Anne's Lace unfolds in the warmth of the mid-morning sun. Black-eyed Susans fill the ditches. Robins have left without a word of farewell. The Chippewa County Fair is only a memory. Another school year has started. All around us are the familiar signs that summer is passing, and soon leaves will turn from green to red and orange. They'll drift to the ground as cool breezes announce the arrival of autumn.

This was an odd summer. It seemed much colder than usual, but perhaps that was due to the brisk temperature in my home. Almost every day I donned the same sweater I had worn all winter. My petunias fulfilled my prophecy that they wouldn't look much different in September from what they did in May. The impatiens next to them grew like weeds, but the petunias failed to produce more than a few new blooms. I transplanted some flowers from the backyard, but some still wait to be moved to a better place where they won't be threatened by the blade of my lawnmower. I didn't finish whacking the tall grass around my spruce trees and probably won't bother with it now. Maybe I'll have more energy come spring.

Miss Peggy, my feline friend, was not pleased with all the noisy traffic on our road, but I told her the guys working on Six Mile will soon be wrapping up their equipment and things will return to normal. She seems to enjoy the appearance of morning sunlight as it filters through my curtains. Lately she hasn't scratched at my bedroom door in her attempt to rouse me from my slumbers.

My outside work is unfinished. I didn't paint my back steps or an old shed. The wood trim around my front door remains as it was when the porcupine chewed it. I didn't bother to slap some white paint on it. Weeds pushed their way through cracks in my cement. I let them grow instead of pulling them up. Ants created little piles of sand in my garage and around my front door. I swept the sand away a few times, but eventually I gave up. Now I merely step around the piles and let the ants carry on.

I did accomplish a few things that had nothing to do with chores. I finished a book of short stories now available for sale. I rearranged this collection of newspaper columns my publisher wants as a future book. I wrote stories for toddlers that may or may not see the light of publication. I finished writing the sequel to the "SideRoad Kids." My summer was filled with words more than deeds.

Unlike the trees, wildflowers, and fields that will rest until spring, my fingers will continue to write. An excerpt from the first line of a poem by Keats haunts me and pushes me forward. "When I have fears that I may cease to be before my pen has gleaned my teeming brain" is always in my thoughts. I've waited too long to commit to paper what was in my mind. Now I rush to finish what I should have started decades ago when age seventy-six seemed a long way off.

Christmas and Chemistry

My former father-in-law loved lemon meringue pies. Many years ago, I decided to bake one for him as a special Christmas gift. My husband, Rick, and I never knew what to get his dad because he always said he didn't want anything. My father's response was the same. When I asked Dad what he wanted for Christmas, he repeatedly said he didn't want anything but, of course, I couldn't wrap an empty box and send it home as a present. Every Christmas throughout my childhood and far into adulthood, Dad got a box of hankies and a pair of brown cotton work gloves. But back to Rick's dad.

I had never attempted to make a lemon meringue pie. However, I considered my lack of expertise only a minor snag and reached for my dependable Betty Crocker's New Picture Cookbook. The directions on page 353 were explicit and easy to follow. I figured even an inexperienced baker wouldn't have any trouble making the pie. However, as I stirred the lemon curd I noticed something strange taking place inside the saucepan. The lovely yellow color was turning green. I was fairly certain green was not the right shade for a lemon pie. With a certain amount of trepidation, I stopped stirring and stuck a spoon into the pan. There was no doubt about the lemony taste. It was delicious. I dismissed my feelings of anxiety and continued stirring until the consistency was perfect.

The pie shell I had baked was cool and waiting to be filled. Ignoring my common sense, I poured that green curd into the shell. I had done a fine job of crimping the crust around the vintage glass pie dish, and the amount of filling was just right. Other than being green, the pie looked scrumptious. When Rick came into the kitchen he asked why I had made a lime pie instead of a lemon one. I explained it was a lemon pie. It just had a different color probably due to the lemons. I suggested he taste the spoonful left in the saucepan but he declined.

"You can't serve that pie," he said. "It's poisonous." I told him he was crazy. I did admit it was the wrong color, but it had a wonderfully tart lemony taste his father would love. I held my ground until Rick looked at the saucepan in the sink. He asked if I had taken a chemistry class in high school. I replied of course not. I pointed out what was obvious to me: Chemistry was for boys, not for girls who loved literature and had no interest in chemistry, geometry, or physics. Then patiently and in great detail, Rick explained that the acid in the lemons had reacted with the aluminum pan changing the bright yellow to a chartreuse green. I wasn't convinced. It hadn't killed me, I explained in my defense, and I doubted it would kill Rick, Sr. Nevertheless, my husband insisted I bin the pie and make a batch of chocolate chip cookies, which is what I did. When we arrived at my in-laws' home in Sterling Heights for the Christmas feast, everyone politely raved about my cookies. I had given Rick strict orders not to mention my disastrous pie.

When the festivities were over and we returned home, I looked at my green lemon dessert destined to go from the countertop to the garbage can. I had to admit a basic knowledge of chemistry was essential if I wanted to become a good cook. So, what did I do? Why, what every other woman worth her salt would have done. I threw out that cheap set of aluminum saucepans. My problem was solved and I never had to open a chemistry textbook. When I purchased an expensive set of stainless steel cookware, I made a surprise treat for my father-in-law. He loved it and relished every bite of my perfectly yellow, perfectly tart, lemon meringue pie.

Many years have passed since that Christmas of long ago. Rick and I divorced, his dad passed away, and now I prefer lemon squares to a lemon pie. Recently I discovered a wonderful recipe that doesn't require cooking. Even if I still used aluminum saucepans, I wouldn't have to fret about the color of the curd. Which only goes to show that if we're willing to wait long enough eventually things turn out the way we hoped they would whether it's something made with lemons or something of much greater importance.

The Silence of My Grandfather Clock

In a corner of my living room stands Uncle Steve's grandfather clock. I was dusting it the other day and remembered a song about a clock that was purchased "on the morn of the day he was born." The song goes on to tell us that it was "too big for a shelf so it stood ninety years on the floor." My uncle's clock wasn't purchased on the day he was born, and it didn't tell him the time for ninety years because it was bought in 1981. However, it did stop on the day he died, May 3, 1993. Its hands tell me it's 4:16 and has been for the past thirty years.

I wasn't as faithful at keeping it going as my uncle had been. He loved that clock and took great pride in it. He knew how to work the chains. He always wore a pair of knit yellow gloves when he pulled the "train" end of the chain that pulls the weights up and winds the clock. The gloves as well as the weights are wrapped in a cloth and stored inside the clock where they'll remain until someone resurrects them. Then the pendulum will tick off the minutes, the chimes will sound the quarter hour, and *tempus fugit* will once again remind us of how quickly time goes by.

When I look at that silent clock, it reminds me of my uncle. I knew him as a man of few words. He was a bachelor and was used to living alone. When he retired, he put a lot of time and effort into his home, built by his father. I visited him one day when I was home from Detroit. It was the first time I had seen the new clock. I remember asking him why he had bought it. His answer was simple. "I always wanted one," he said. "The pendulum reminds me that nothing in life is stationary." I was sitting on the couch across from him. He pointed to the clock and said, "One day, that will be yours. It will come with this house. Take good care of everything." Little did we know the sorrow that was to come.

Every day when I sit at my desk and glance at that clock, I remember the way things were and how much they have changed. In a way, the clock is a symbol of change. As it stands sentry, silent and oblivious to its surroundings, I can't help but wonder what Uncle Steve would make of all the hours that have passed since he's been gone. Would he ask if the country we live in today is the same one he went to war for? Would his Wildcat buddies who died in World War II be proud of our nation? Would he look at his military uniform, his honorable discharge papers, and the photos of him in the Philippines and ask what happened? Would he want to know when we stopped being a "melting pot" and began showing hostility to legal immigrants and openly fighting each other over political and social issues?

As a man of few words, he might never have offered an opinion. He might even have ignored everything and gone about his own business. In summer, he would have worked in his garden. In winter, he would have taken his fish shanty to the frozen lake and spent hours fishing for perch. When his day was done and the dishes were washed and put away, I think he would have played his violin and thought about the old days. When his clock chimed ten, he would have climbed his stairs and made ready for bed. Only then he might have wondered when and why it all went so wrong.

I'd Be Lost Without My Compass

Last fall I went for a walk in the field behind my home. I walked a little farther than I intended and ended up in the woods. It didn't take long before I was turned around. I never thought about putting a compass in my pocket. After all, I grew up on these twenty acres and as a kid, I never got lost. I suppose I should have remembered that nature reclaims its own when left alone. No cattle have been in our fields for more than fifty years.

When I was young, our milk cows grazed the grass around the barn and in the pastures, and they ate whatever they found in the woods. My siblings and I used the woods as our playground. We made temporary structures from the limbs of dead trees and branches as walls. In the fall, we collected colorful leaves. It never occurred to us we might get lost as we searched for the ever phantom hazelnut tree.

But the cows are long gone, the fences rotted away, the woods have become a tangled mass of tamarack and spruce trees, and it only takes a minute to get disorientated. For some unknown reason, I was trying to find our 1952 Chevy. When it died, Dad hooked a chain to the tractor and dragged the car to the woods and forgot about it. When I was young, it was easy to find because it was just inside the fence. The cows ignored it, but for me it was wonderful. I didn't find the car, but thinking about it brought back memories.

When I headed for the woods my first stop was always that Chevy. I taught myself to drive. True, I never left the field, but I prided myself on never getting into an accident either. I turned the steering wheel to the left and right, turned on the radio, rolled down the windows, and headed for St. Ignace and the ferry. In my mind, I drove all the way to Detroit. When I got tired of driving, I rolled up the windows, turned off the radio, and went as deep into the woods as I dared.

I never took a compass because I didn't need one. I followed the fence or the cows' path and when it ran out, I made my own. The woods were not thick, and it was easy to find my way back to the open field. If I was gone too long, my parents would say I should have taken a compass with me just in case I got lost. I told them I didn't know how to read one so Dad showed me. As a child, I had no more idea how to make sense of the needle pointing north than I did of how the earth spun on its axis. What if I didn't want to go north? What would I do then, I'd ask.

After a while, my parents gave up and gave me a whistle if I needed help. I don't recall ever using it. I came across it the other day when I was rummaging through drawers. That's when I found Dad's compass. It's about three inches tall and the top unscrews. Dad kept matches in the hollow cylinder. I also found a small brass compass. It was meant to pin on a hunter's jacket, but I don't think it was ever used because it was still in its original box.

Finding those compasses reminded me they are still important today. Smartphones are wonderful creations, but if we enter a "dead zone" the likelihood of getting a signal is remote. It's easy to get turned around as I discovered when I walked only a short distance into the woods. I had no point of reference, and no idea where I was. It took only a minute for panic to set in as night began to fall. Golly, I thought. I have no compass, and I'm getting cold. I'll probably die in my own woods, and the turkey vultures will pick my bones clean before anyone finds me. Okay, that's a slight exaggeration, but if you've ever been lost, you know how easy it is to panic.

When I was in town a few days later, I stopped at a sporting goods store and asked if they sold compasses. One young clerk had no idea what I was referring to, but another clerk found four. I asked if there was much call for them. She said my request was the first she had heard in a long time. Seasoned hunters or hikers know the value of a compass. Like my Dad, they know that faithful needle pointing north will guide them back to safety.

The next time I go for a walk in my woods, I'll be sure to pin the little compass on my jacket. I won't have to whistle and pretend I'm not afraid as I hunt for an opening in the trees pointing the way home. Or maybe I'll just stick to the road. It's not very exciting, but at least I don't have to worry about getting lost. Sometimes you have to admit that erring on the side of caution is just good common sense.

The Sand in My Hourglass Runs Low

Although advanced in years, I never thought of myself as old until a dentist pointed it out to me. This morning when I walked down my road, the realization that the sand in my hourglass is, indeed, running low, hit me full force. For the first time in three years, I "took the hill" meaning I walked down one hill and up the other. I felt like Rocky when he ran up the steps of the Philadelphia art museum. He was young and robust and took those seventy-two stone steps like a champ. I am old and arthritic. I always walk with ski poles to maintain balance, but regardless, I cheered as I crested the steep hill.

I saw cracks in the asphalt and weeds struggling to grow between them. They showed me that nature reclaims its own. As I walked down the hill towards the river, I felt the eyes of my deceased cousin boring into my back and wondered how many times he had watched me from his home atop the hill. When I reached the bridge, I paused. Mist rising from the water was like a pastoral scene painted by one of the masters. The "View of Richmond Hill and Bridge" by Turner was not a replica of what I saw, but the serenity I felt might have equaled the feelings of the artist.

The beauty of the scene reminded me that I am old and appreciate the simplicity of nature. The clouds of mist from the river floated high into the air. I shaded my eyes from the rising sun and followed them as they rose higher and higher until disappearing among the tree tops. Then I examined the spiderwebs along the railing and observed a spider busily weaving her gossamer trap. I thought of the unseen life flourishing underneath the water. A tiny sparrow landed on the railing, but quickly flew away. My gaze followed her as she sought the safety of a spruce tree. In my mind, I heard the McCrary boys, Rex and Gordon and Roger, laughing and yelling a greeting as they ran down the hill towards the river for their early morning swim.

As I walked past the barn built by Uncle John, I recalled how high the mow was compared to ours and how pristine the cement floor was to our dirt one. His cows were kept in place by stanchions. Ours had chains around their necks allowing them greater freedom of movement. I remembered the pig pen my uncle had built and moved from place to place as the grass turned to mud. I saw the forest surrounding me and knew milk cows would never again spend lazy summer days in what had been their pastures, nor would I pick blueberries in the overgrown brush.

Yes, I thought, I am old. However, it is not my physical body that bruises easily, but my spirit. It yearns for a more sensible time when neighbors helped, instead of shot, each other. For a time when people could discuss politics in a rational manner. When children could play outside without fear of being kidnapped. When summer was a time to ride bicycles, build treehouses, swim in the river, pick berries, play softball in front yards, and stay outside until sunset.

My hourglass is almost empty. I may never again "take the hill" but for a few brief moments this morning, my step was light, my heart was young.

About the Author

Sharon M. Kennedy lives in Michigan's Upper Peninsula on the land of her youth. As an opinion writer for Gannett Media, her newspaper columns reflect a keen observation of people and their experiences. Whether humorous, serious, or poignant, she records events and situations relatable to individuals of various ages. Kennedy has the remarkable ability to communicate with readers as if they were sitting at her kitchen table, sharing a cup of coffee and a laugh with her.

Enjoy U.P. Stories from the View of a Yooper

Join us for a trip through Michigan's rural Upper Peninsula in this collection of fictional short stories. Let the characters of *View from the SideRoad* surprise you with their resilience, humor, and unpredictability. Whether it's a sailor who shuns water, an old maid who wants to shoot her cats, or a man who keeps his lover in the junk drawer, the stories range from witty to wry to weepy. Sharon is a master of the short form. As readers of her newspaper column and previous collections will attest, she never disappoints.

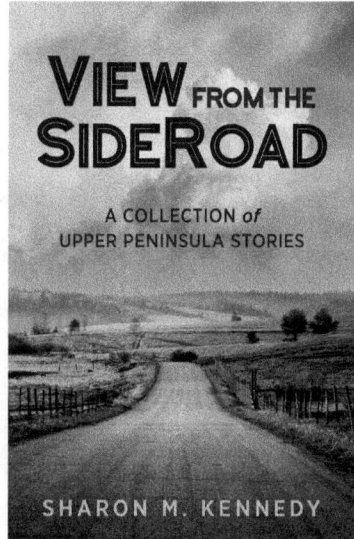

Her stories will keep you turning the pages and thirsting for more.

"Penned by Sharon Kennedy, a hidden gem in the wilds of Michigan's Eastern Upper Peninsula, this book is a fine collection of humorous, satirical, and poignant stories."
>   --Jim Dwyer, Writer, *Mackinac Journal*

"*View from the SideRoad* weaves vivid tales with warmth and humor. The author really knows how to captivate the reader with tantalizing stories."
>   --Jill Lowe Brumwell, Author of *Drummond Island: History, Folklore, and Early People*

"Sharon Kennedy is one of the Upper Peninsula's premier writers. A well-read columnist in the Eastern U.P., she has turned her attention to writing books and U.P. literature is the better for it. Her stories are reminiscent of Cully Gage's, *Northwoods Readers*, but with her own spin and style."
>   --Mikel Classen, Author of *True Tales: Forgotten History of Michigan's Upper Peninsula*, recipient of Charles Follo Award

Learn more at www.AuthorSharonKennedy.com
From Modern History Press

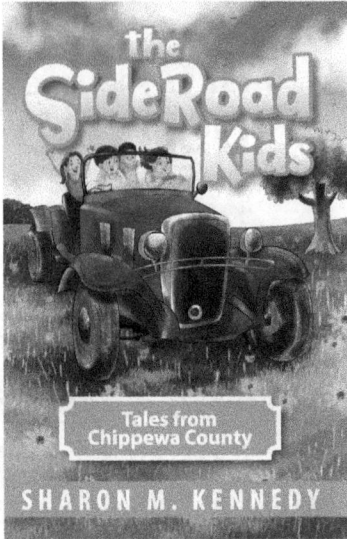

The SideRoad Kids follows a group of boys and girls as they enter the sixth grade in a small town in Michigan's Upper Peninsula during 1957 - 58. This meandering collection of loosely-connected short stories is often humorous, poignant, and sometimes mysterious. Laugh as the kids argue over Halloween treats handed out in Brimley. Recall Dorothy's Hamburgers in Sault Ste. Marie. Follow a Sugar Island snowshoe trail as the kids look for Christmas trees. Wonder what strange blue smoke at Dollar Settlement signifies. Discover the magic hidden in April snowflakes. Although told by the kids, adults will remember their own childhood as they read about Flint, Candy, Squeaky, Katie, and their friends.

"Katie, Blew, Squeaky, and Daisy grew up on farms instead of high rises and used their imagination instead of fancy gadgets to make their own fun. An entertaining read for youngsters. And parents, you might enjoy a nostalgic flashback as well. I know I did."
                    --Allia Zobel-Nolan, author of *Cat Confessions*

"The stories in *The SideRoad Kids* are often humorous. However, underlying them is a sensitive awareness that being a kid, rural or urban, then or now, is not easy. This is an enjoyable read that will enlighten today's kids about the past and rekindle memories for older readers."
                    --Jon C. Stott, author of *Paul Bunyan in Michigan*

"Sharon's stories capture the essence of childhood and growing up in a small community. The antics of The SideRoad Kids will keep you entertained and take you back to a simpler time."
--Renee Glass, Senior Production Artist, *Mackinac Journal*

Learn more at www.AuthorSharonKennedy.com
From Modern History Press

www.ingramcontent.com/pod-product-compliance
Lightning Source LLC
Chambersburg PA
CBHW060433090426
42733CB00011B/2255